TOPMARKS

TOPMARKS

A Nautical Quiz Book

Compiled and written by

Bill Beavis

NAUTICAL

First published in Great Britain 1986 by
NAUTICAL BOOKS
an imprint of Conway Maritime Press Ltd
24 Bride Lane, Fleet Street
London EC4Y 8DR
ISBN 0 85177 418 0

Line illustrations by the author

Typeset by C R Barber & Partners Ltd, Fort William
Printed in Great Britain by The Bath Press, Bath

The examples in the 'In Your Judgement' series were taken from two excellent books on maritime law: *The Law for Small Boats* by Andrew Phelan, and the *Sea Lawyer* by Brian Calwell.

QUESTIONS

NAMESAKES

1 A fictional sailor has had an island recently named after him. Who?
2 What knot is named after a Portsmouth Dockyard rigger?
3 Which international yacht race honours a yacht which fought on both sides in the American Civil War?
4 Film actress Mae West gave her name to . . . ?
5 Kaiser Wilhelm gave his name to . . . ?
6 A navigable stretch of water is named after which Portuguese explorer?
7 Which British yachtsman has a rock and a mountain named after his boat?
8 Miss Fanny Adams gave her name to . . . ?
9 Park Avenue gave its name to which piece of equipment?
10 Which doctor has recently had a knot named after him?
11 Which British yachtsman has a flower named after him?
12 Which British admiral has a drink named after his trousers?
13 Jimmy Green gave his name to a . . . ?
14 What name of an eastern seaport suggests abduction?
15 Friedrich Heinrich . . . gave his name to which coastal current?
16 Hydrographer Thomas Hurd is immortalised by what feature?
17 Objects on a ship's binnacle commemorate the achievement of two British scientists. What are their names?
18 Which writer of sea adventure stories took a part of a ship for his pseudonym?
19 Which fictional character of Captain Marryat writes a column in a British daily newspaper?
20 Which saint has given his name to a discharge of static electricity?
21 What item in a boat's canvas immortalises an America's Cup skipper?
22 The leadsman's call inspired the pen name of which literary figure?

23 Who, when his Bill was dropped, stood up in the British House of Commons, called his Parliamentary colleagues 'villains' and shook his fist at the Speaker, but lived to see the object of this Bill on half the world's shipping?
24 Which esteemed British engineer designed and built harbours and canals and yet is remembered chiefly today for a stump sticking out of a rock?
25 Which navy commander carried out a brutal and punitive raid against the French and whose name has become synonymous with a good hiding?
26 Which American admiral has a dance named after him?

Answers on page 71

SPOT THE PLOT

Give the name of the novels, and their authors, which have these plots.

1 An upper-class English family are invited on a yacht cruise which ends dramatically when they are wrecked on a Pacific Island. The butler who has been brought along to wait on the family emerges as the most competent member of the group and everyone is made subservient to his iron rule. The daughter falls in love with him. However, once they are rescued the family try to treat him as a servant once more.
2 A helper at a mission has to flee when the soldiers come. She joins a boat in an advanced state of disrepair skippered by a drunk. But with her strong Christian convictions she reforms the man, wills their escape and persuades him to take an active part in the war.
3 Two hundred migrant workers are returning home with two year's wages made up in silver coins. The ship they travel in is commanded by an honest but totally unimaginative captain – so unimaginative that he hasn't the wit to avoid the storm whose signs are obvious. Great damage and injury is done by

the storm but the worst victims are the migrant workers who are thrown violently from side to side in the ship's hold. In consequence all the silver coins are spilled. The captain's solution to the upset this causes is to collect the money and share it out equally.

4 A group of early conservationists turn militant when a party going on aboard a charter boat is upsetting a nesting bird. They cut the boat adrift. A protracted chase ensues and ends happily when the charter party, the clear villains of the piece, are wrecked on a sandbank and have to be rescued by their tormentors.

5 A fisherman alone in a small boat hooks a fish which carries him out to sea. For two days he fights the fish, talking to it all the while. Eventually he harpoons it, the biggest fish he has ever caught. Too big for the boat, he lashes it alongside but by the time he makes harbour the sharks have taken their share and all that remains is a skeleton.

Answers on pages 71-72

IN YOUR JUDGEMENT (1)

A sailing barge had anchored in the River Medina. At low water she took the ground at the edge of the channel. Soon afterwards, a motor boat came up the channel, which in this vicinity was a mere thirty feet wide with about six feet of depth at the maximum, and struck the upstanding fluke of the sailing barge's anchor and sank. At the subsequent court hearing the sailing barge skipper denied all responsibility. He said he had authority to anchor in his position, that the motor boat had no business navigating with just a foot of water under her keel, and if her crew had bothered to look they would have seen the barge's chain cable snaking across the mud, a clear indication of where the anchor lay. Who then in your opinion was to blame?

Answer on page 71

POWER TO HAND

Can you state the mechanical advantage in the following?

(a)

(b)

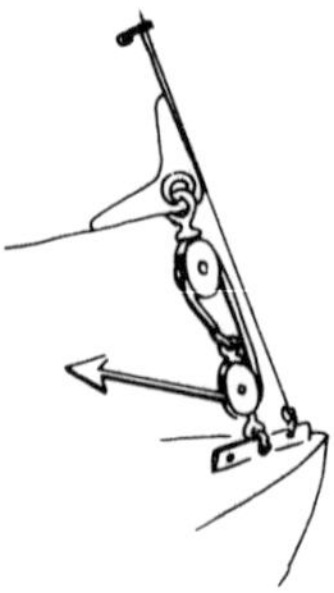

(c)

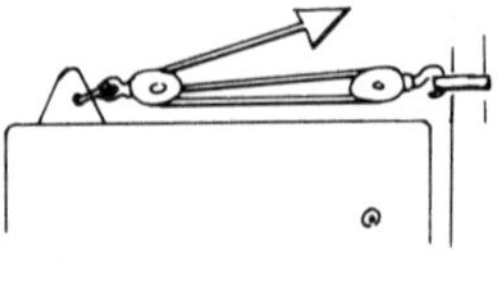

(d)

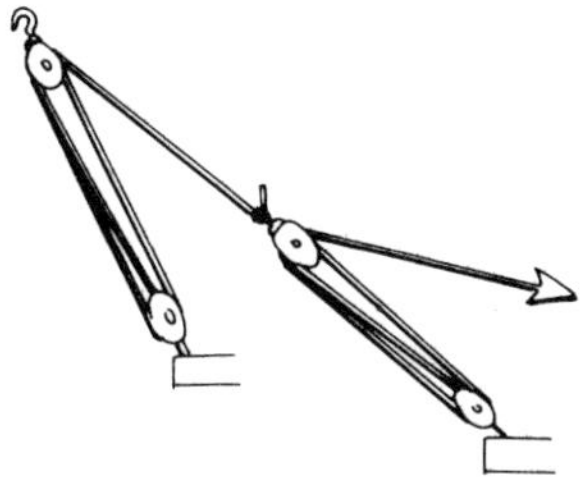

(e)

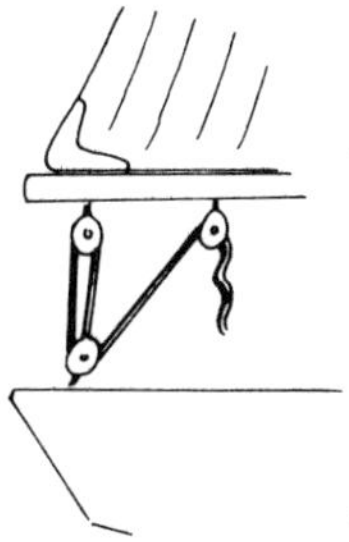

(f)

(g)

(h)

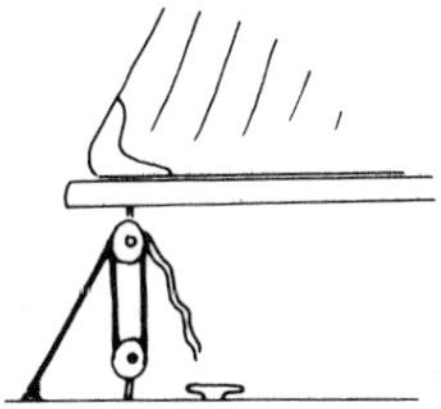

(i)

(j)

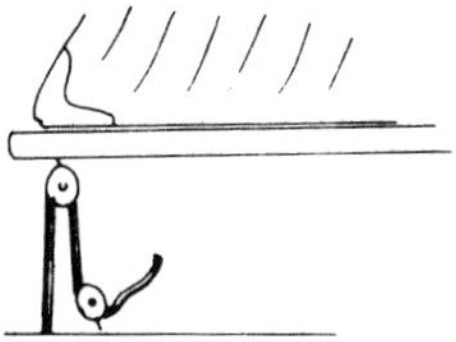

(k)

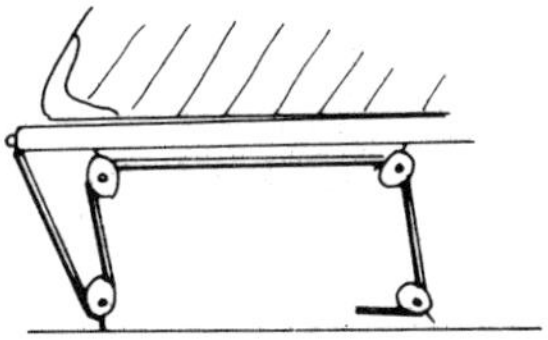

(l)

Answers on page 72

WHERE DOES SHE COME FROM?

Port Distinguishing Letters for fishing boats have been used for almost a hundred years. Each letter or sequence of letters gives an indication of the port at which the vessel is registered. Below are listed two dozen letters; can you tell where they belong?

Scotland	*Wales*	*Ireland*	*England*
AA	AB	B	BK
DS	CF	C	E
FR	CO	D	FY
GW	LA	G	GY
INS	MH	WD	MN
	SA	Y	SSS

Answers on page 72

SMOKE TRAIL

The ship is travelling on an easterly course and her speed is 10 knots. The smoke 'feather' is 15 miles (i.e. 15 knots). Can you tell what is the direction and speed of the wind?

Answers on page 72

DO YOU REMEMBER WHEN... ? (1)

You remember the events, but in what year did they occur?

1 New anti-seasickness pill Stugeron available; Brighton Marina opened; new lightvessel CHANNEL on station
2 *Suhaili* became the first boat to circumnavigate the world without stopping; Maiden voyage of *QE2*; first Southampton Boat Show; Exeter Maritime Museum opened
3 Tougher rabies laws introduced in UK with maximum fine of £1000; Spithead Review; Major Bill Tilman disappears in South Atlantic; Freedom rig makes its debut; Traffic Separation Scheme introduced in Dover Strait
4 Maurice Griffiths retires after 41 years as editor of *Yachting Monthly*; Donald Campbell in fatal crash in *Bluebird K7*; *Torrey Canyon* runs aground on Seven Stones rocks; Arthur Ransome dies; *Practical Boat Owner* magazine launched; Francis Chichester completes circumnavigation in *Gypsy Moth IV*
5 Penlee lifeboat disaster; Westerly Marine Construction in hands of Receiver; Yachtsman/author has Falkland Island pilot book classified; *Mary Rose* raised off Portsmouth
6 *Malcolm Miller* joins STA fleet; Rodney Pattison and Ian Macdonald-Smith win Gold Medal at Mexico Olympics; Geoffrey Williams wins OSTAR in *Sir Thomas Lipton*; remains of *Mary Rose* found by divers
7 HM Coastguard announce cliff-top look-outs to be phased out; Small Ships Register introduced; Chatham Dockyard closes; David Scott Cowper begins round-the-world attempt in ex-Dungeness lifeboat

Answers on page 73

DO YOU REMEMBER WHEN. . . ? (2)

1 Edward Heath's yacht *Morning Cloud* sinks off the Owers; *Gumboots* becomes first British winner of the One Ton Cup; *Courageous* beats Australia's *Southern Cross* at Newport, RI

2 Angus Primrose drowned off USA; Capt John Illingworth dies; Phil Weld wins OSTAR in *Moxie*

3 Largest single-handed yacht *Vendredi Treize* competes in OSTAR; Uffa Fox dies; Fathom disappears from British Admiralty charts; Dougal Robertson and family adrift in Pacific after yacht is sunk by a whale

4 Operation Drake sets sail; First East Coast Boat Show; World's most serious oil pollution incident occurs when *Amoco Cadiz* is wrecked in Brittany

5 Chancellor introduces 25 per cent VAT on yachts and equipment; *Crossbow* becomes first yacht to break the 30-knot barrier; First transatlantic race for fully crewed multihulls

6 HMS *Belfast* transferred to The Belfast Trust; Chay Blyth sets off to sail the 'wrong way' around the world in *British Steel*; After multiple sinkings on Varne, Trinity House take unprecedented step of marking wrecks with two lightvessels and fourteen light buoys

7 First Round-the-World Race begins; RYA co-operates with Department of Trade and introduces new Yachtmaster syllabus; Maurice and Marilyn Bailey rescued after three months adrift in Pacific; Clare Francis crosses Atlantic single-handed in *Gulliver G*

Answers on page 73

SAY THAT AGAIN

Most sailors pride themselves on making themselves understood abroad. But how would you get on with these?

1 *Buitenboordskraan* is Dutch for:
- a deck scrubber
- b seacock
- c answering pendant

2 *Strapuntino* is Italian for:
- a sculling oar
- b snap shackle
- c mattress

3 *Carlinga superior no convez, para um mastro basculante* is Portuguese for:
- a roller headsail reefing gear
- b tabernacle
- c winch handle

4 *Croissant* is French for:
- a a boom claw
- b a ship's biscuit
- c a station pointer

5 *Overstag gaan, wenden, door de wind gaan* is Dutch for:
- a Running before the wind
- b Give way to vessels on starboard tack
- c 'Ready about!'

6 *Fockausbaumer* is German for:
- a whisker pole
- b measurement certificate
- c corkscrew

Answer on page 73

WE'VE GOT PROBLEMS (1)

Sidney is in double trouble. His wife told him she didn't want the boat parked on the lawn and now the weight of it has sunk a keel block through the drains. (That is Sidney's wife's washing-up water jetting skyward.)

The problem: how is Sidney (singlehanded) going to lift five tons of boat so that he can insert a fresh keel block and repair his drain? He dare not hire a mobile crane for the damage it would do to the lawn. Nor can he use his car jack because it is meant for Minis and Minis don't weigh five tons.

Answer on page 73

CROSSWORD (1)

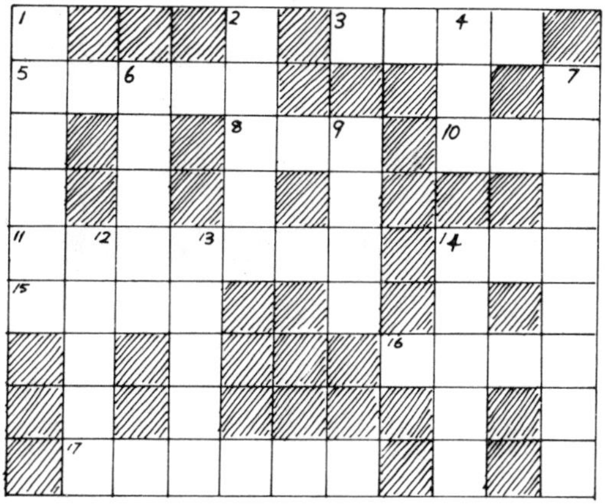

Across

3 Pukka Sahibs' way to travel (4)
5 Hammers out a warning from on high (5)
8 Some manage with one (3)
10 Drift's partner (3)
11 A quick fix (7)
14 Sailor's acknowledgement (3)
15 Better than rolling (4)
16 Seen in Sweden (4)
17 Not for the navigating purist (6)

Down

1 All hung up (6)
2 You couldn't dance on this one (5)
4 Stops all radio chat (3)
6 Early shantymen used them (5)
7 An uncomfortable passage (8)
9 Their departure can be worse than their presence (4)
12 Gets the message across (5)
13 Twice used 'unrestrictedly' (1,4)
14 Wrecks and rocks are more dangerous . . . (5)

Answers on page 74

SILHOUETTES

(a)

(b)

(c)

(d)

(e)

(f)

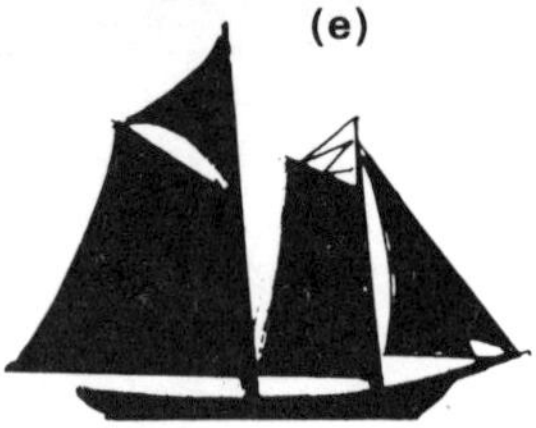

(g)

(h)

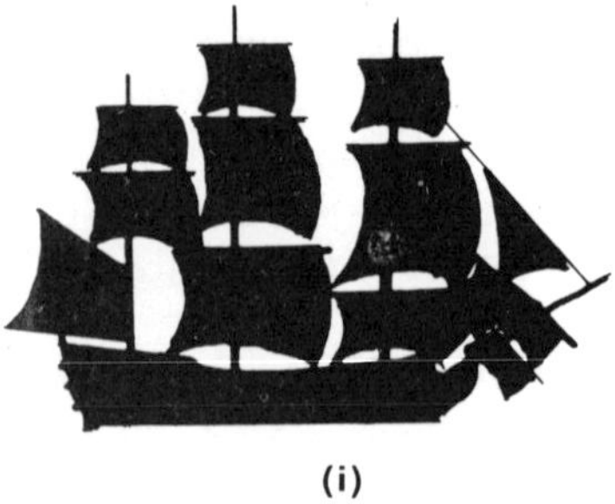

(i)

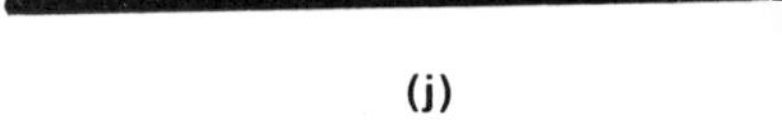

(j)

These are the silhouettes of ten famous vessels. Can you recognise them?

Answers on page 74

NAUTICAL ACRONYMS

What do the following stand for?

1	TSDY	**11**	SAR
2	LASH	**12**	Ro/Ro
3	MOCRA	**13**	LANBY
4	CQR	**14**	RNR
5	MLWN	**15**	IYRU
6	YBDSA	**16**	IMO
7	VLCC	**17**	SINS
8	RNSA	**18**	RFA
9	BACAT	**19**	ACV
10	RORC	**20**	OSTAR

Answers on page 74

IN YOUR JUDGEMENT (2)

After collision with another vessel (there was no evidence of negligence) a motor yacht sank in a fairway. The owner immediately contacted his insurers and the harbour master to say he was abandoning the vessel as a total loss. The harbour master went out to survey the wreck and discovered she was causing an obstruction. He ordered divers to place explosives in the wreck and blow her up and then sued the boat's owner for payment of expenses. Did the owner have to pay?

Answer on page 75

WHOSE ARE THEY?

It is your first morning in a sail loft. You arrive at work to find the boss has run off to Bora Bora with the girl who delivers exhaust parts. On the floor are four bundles of sails – all unmarked! Your job, before the 'phones start ringing, is to identify the four boats to which the sails belong.

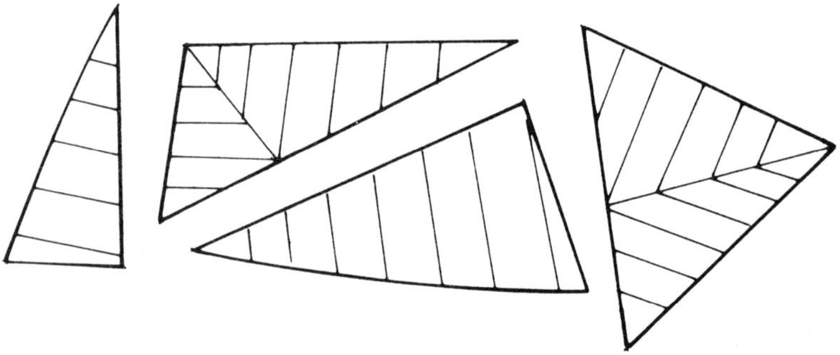

2

1

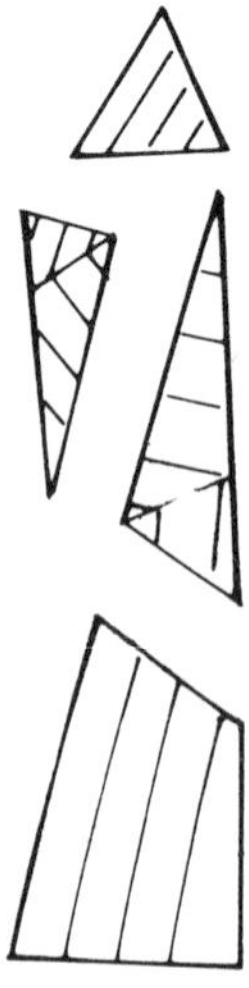

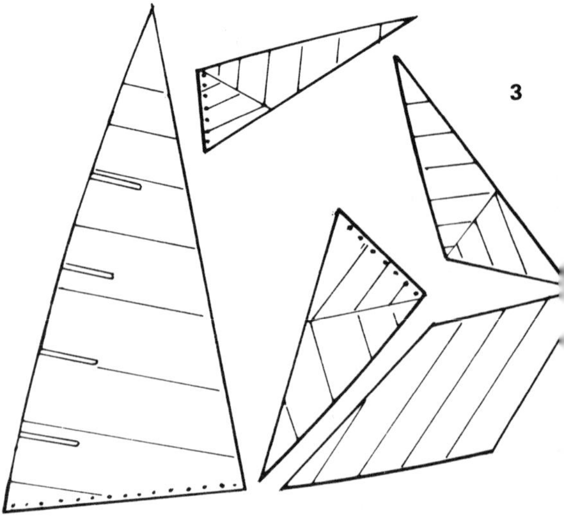

3

4

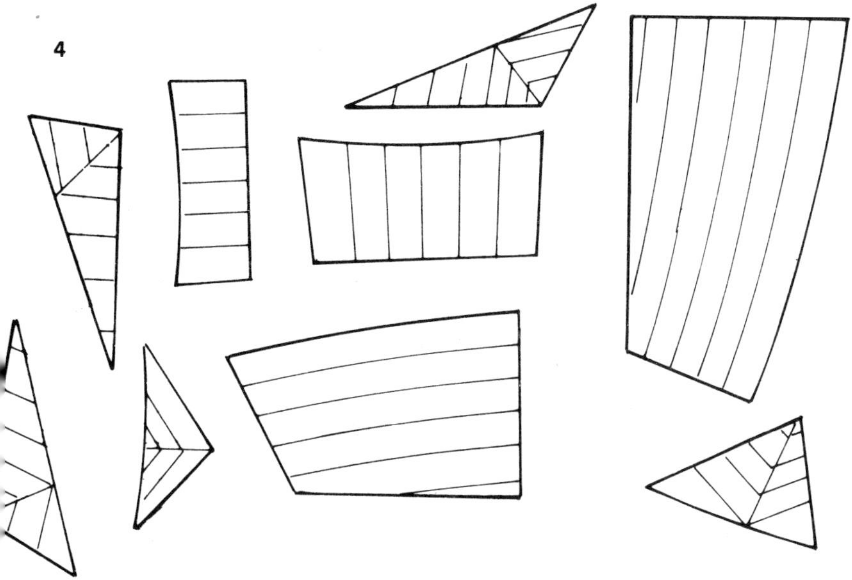

Answer on page 75

WE'VE GOT PROBLEMS (2)

Sidney has been left to park the trailer but the launching slip is too steep and the trailer too heavy for him to move alone. All he has done has been to chock off the wheel with a brick. With no outside help and no equipment, can you suggest a way he could get the trailer up the slope before the tide engulfs them?

Answer on page 75

IN YOUR JUDGEMENT (3)

A 100-ton motor yacht picked up a pilot at Poole Bar with the warning that the engines were giving trouble. Hearing this, the pilot suggested it might be wise to have the pilot launch standby. They proceeded but just as they reached the seaward end of the training bank, which lies to the west of the entrance channel, the engines failed completely. It was a fine afternoon with a slight easterly wind. The tide, which with the existence of the training bank runs more or less up and down the channel, was flooding. The pilot and the skipper discussed what to do and left the bridge to consult with the owner, a retired navy captain, who was in his cabin. The question was whether to anchor (as a precaution the anchor had already been walked out) and effect the repair which the engineer estimated would take about two hours, or use the pilot launch to tow her into her berth at Poole quay. In the end it was decided to use the launch to take her up to the quay. There was some difficulty in securing the launch and twice the towline broke. They were then joined by a workboat whose crew assisted in the tow until the yacht was manoeuvred inside the harbour where the pilot launch was properly secured alongside for the tow to the quay.

Subsequently, the workboat crew claimed salvage. They argued that the yacht was too far west in the channel and was drifting onto a lee shore. The holding ground was poor, they said, and (contrary to the court's finding) there was a freshening wind. They also maintained that without their help the yacht would have gone ashore and been broken up by evening.

Were the crew correct in their assertions?

Answer on page 76

ODDBALLS

Described here are some unusual vessels, in some cases out-and-out freaks while others have unique, if not slightly cranky, features. For some answers the name of the vessel is required, for others it is the class.

1 A pulling or rowing boat which has two oars on one side and three shorter oars on the other
2 The ship, designed to abolish seasickness, which had its main saloon slung in gimbals
3 A dugout canoe purchased from a Canadian Indian, decked over and then sailed around the world
4 A warship with three decks of oars
5 A submarine with an aircraft and hangar
6 Boats whose principal design requirement was that they could be stacked one inside the other and be more stable when loaded
7 A ship with hinged sections which could undulate with the waves
8 A catamaran with solid sails
9 An ocean racing boat which used depleted uranium for ballast
10 A seven-masted schooner
11 An amphibious jeep which was sailed, and driven, around the world
12 A single-handed yacht so large it employed closed circuit television so the skipper could keep an eye on the sails
13 A royal yacht built in Scotland with a completely round hull
14 A trimaran whose floats fold in to reduce berthing charges and permit navigation on canals
15 A boat which can be sailed both forwards and backwards
16 Double-ended warships built so the enemy wouldn't know which way they were going
17 A cross-Channel ship which ran on rollers

Answers on page 76

SPOT THE STRUCTURES

(a)

(b)

(c)

(d)

(e)

(f)

(g)

(h)

Can you name these unique, largely military, structures?

Answers on page 76

WE'VE GOT PROBLEMS (3)

Sidney has made his own mooring, a lorry tyre filled with concrete. He prided himself on the wisdom of this choice because, being round, he was able to wheel it down to the foreshore. Ah, but what he hadn't considered was how to get it into the workboat and motor it out to the mooring space he has been allocated. It is much too heavy for him to lift and, as he got up especially early, there isn't anyone around who can help him.

Answer on page 77

SINGLE-HANDING CAN GET YOU THAT WAY

Can you identify these single-handers from their antics and utterances?

1 The Englishman who confirmed Australians' long held suspicions about Poms and their bathing habits, when he announced on his arrival in Sydney that he endeavoured to take a bath once every three months 'whether he needed it or not'

2 The lady who claims to make all her tropical crossings in a crash helmet and a nightie

3 The soldier turned sailor who attracted the attention of a Russian ship by firing his gun at the bridge

4 The Latvian who crossed the Pacific in a decked-over inshore boat using home-made log, chronometer and a sextant whose vernier was a modified woodscrew turning in the teeth of a hacksaw blade, and on passage overstayed in a group of islands not even mentioned on his home-drawn charts

5 The lady circumnavigator who admitted that she occasionally got lost in Woolworths and then gave the claim currency by confusing latitude with longitude

6 The unfortunate man who found the pressures of single-handed racing too much, and sent a series of radio position reports with deliberate errors of many thousands of miles

7 The extrovert well ahead in a single-handed race who suddenly became disenchanted, announced that 'racing was an insult to the sea', retired and took himself off to Tahiti

8 The New Zealand hairdresser who crossed and re-crossed the Atlantic because, he said, he wanted to give his new hair-transplant method a thorough test

9 The Welsh-born sailor who claims to have played chess with his three-legged dog

10 The former brush salesman from Bournemouth who attempted to sail a 19-foot boat through the North West Passage, overwintered in the Arctic and married an Eskimo

11 The ex-car worker from the Midlands who went on to become awarded for his single-handed achievements but whose first trans-Atlantic crossing was less auspicious. Believing his landfall to be the West Indies, he sailed into the mouth of the Amazon, couldn't understand why the water 'turned green' and spent a number of days teaching Amazonian indians how to play golf on the mud flats before contracting dysentery and being carted off to a maternity hospital for treatment

12 The man who, after capsizing three times off Cape Horn, came ashore in New Zealand crippled with a knee injury and, when asked why he was attempting a second circumnavigation in the opposite direction replied that 'he was doing it to unwind'

13 The American sea-captain with five transatlantic crossings behind him who decided at the age of sixty that it was time to go short-handed and advertised for a wife. The couple were married in a pier-head ceremony and set off on their honeymoon attempting the next crossing

Answers on page 77

COLOURFUL, BUT WHAT DO THEY MEAN?

Here are a number of colourful expressions frequently heard at sea. Can you give their meanings?

1 A bone in her teeth
2 Channel fever
3 Parish rigged
4 Charley Noble
5 Honey boat
6 Fiddler's green
7 Soldier's wind
8 Lubber's line
9 Boxing the compass
10 Arming the lead
11 A Handy Billy
12 Mother Carey's chickens
13 Paddy's hurricane
14 Rogue's yarn

Answers on pages 77-78

ROPE TRICKS

Here are ten operations involving rope, wire or small stuff, and all ending with 'ing'. What are they?

(a)

(b)

(c)

(d)

(e)

(f)

(g)

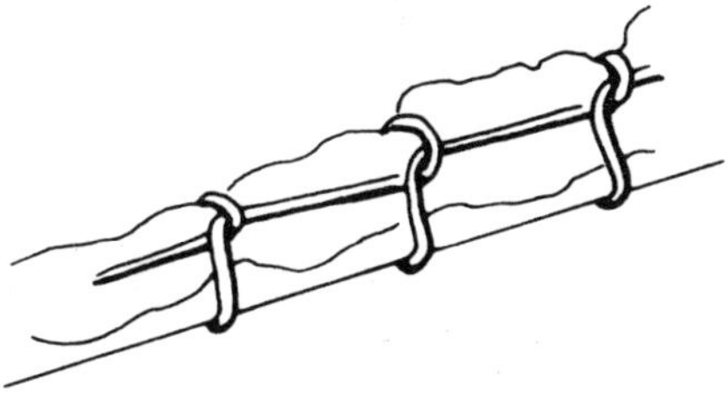

(h)

(i)

(j)

Answers on page 78

JUMBLE!

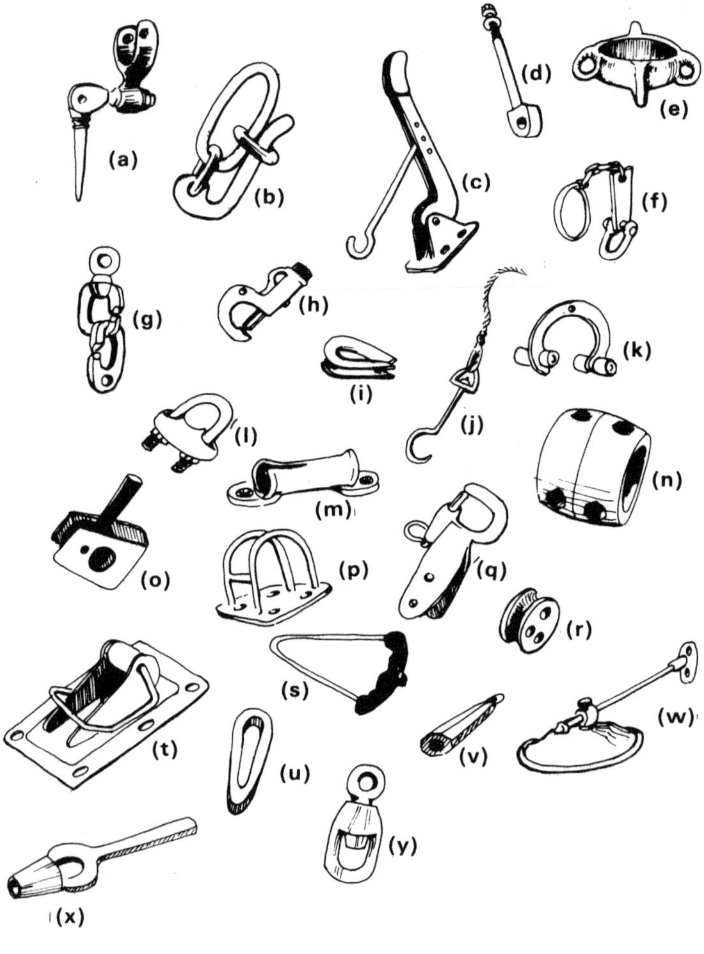

You have been asked to run the chandlery stall at the lifeboat jumble sale. All sorts of stuff have been dumped on your table and you now have to label and identify each one.

Answers on page 78

FIRSTS!

Here is the achievement, but what was the name of the vessel?

1 First yacht to hoist a spinnaker
2 First ship to make a commercial run down the North West Passage
3 First ship to win the Blue Riband Atlantic Trophy
4 First submarine to sail under the North Pole
5 First steam turbine vessel
6 First large British yacht to adopt the Bermudian rig
7 First inflatable with a rigid bottom
8 First cross-Channel catamaran
9 First nuclear-powered commercial ship
10 First vessel to use steam propulsion commercially
11 First 'all big-gun' battleship
12 First warship to be sunk by a guided missile
13 First US Navy warship to be captured at sea for 156 years
14 First ship to cross the Atlantic entirely under its own steam
15 First boat actually designed for saving life at sea

Answers on page 79

IN YOUR JUDGEMENT (4)

A new ship was being made ready to launch. The blocks had been removed and a river buoy, which was in the way of the launching operation, was cleared. Shortly before the ceremony, a yacht came into the river and dropped anchor and in the process fouled the ground chain of the buoy which had been pulled aside. She remained stuck in the launch path. The shipbuilders sent a message to the yacht's owner saying he was in the way of the launch and that he should take immediate steps to move. He refused. The launch was delayed while a second request was made to the yacht to slip its anchor and leave. It was explained that the blocks holding the ship had been removed, and once removed the blocks could not be replaced. The launch would have to go ahead and, unless the yacht moved, she could be damaged. The yacht owner replied that his anchor was fouled because of the shipyard's actions and that he would not move. Later that day the ship was launched and, as predicted, the yacht was damaged.

Who was to blame?

Answer on page 79

SAILING INTO LITERATURE

1 What was the name of Davis's boat in Erskine Childers' *The Riddle of the Sands*?

2 In Jules Verne's *Thirty Thousand Leagues Under the Sea*, the name of the submarine was?

3 What was the name of Captain Ahab's ship in Herman Melville's *Moby Dick*?

4 Author R. H. Dana served in two ships and he mentions them both in his part autobiography *Two Years Before the Mast*. What were they called?

5 Arthur Ransome had a yacht built in Riga and he sailed her extensively in the Baltic. It was even featured in the title of one of his books. What was she called?

6 In Neil Munro's *Para Handy and Other Tales*, what was the name of the steam puffer?

7 In what ship did Able Seaman Ralph Rackstraw serve?

8 The Flower class corvette in Nicholas Monsarrat's *The Cruel Sea* was called?

9 What was the name of the schooner which sailed to *Treasure Island*?

10 Alastair Maclean's novel about life in the Russian convoys during World War II has the name of the ship as its title. What is it?

11 In *Brown on Resolution* by C. S. Forrester, what was the name of the German cruiser?

12 Captain Pugwash's ship is . . . ?

Answers on page 79

THERE IS A WORD FOR IT

Here are the actions; can you supply the correct words which describe them?

1 The boom gybes but the upper half of the sail does not
2 The wind catches the sail on the wrong side
3 The boat is held head to wind
4 In a gaff-rigged boat the action of lowering the peak and hauling up the tack, both at the same time
5 Hauling a sail to windward to turn or stop the vessel
6 To cast off a sheet quickly so that the sail flaps in the wind
7 Sailing the boat with headsail to port and mainsail to starboard (or vice versa)
8 Sailing close-hauled but never pinching and keeping the sails filled and pulling well
9 The air flow from one sail striking the lee side of the other
10 Carrying too much sail for the present wind condition
11 Sailing across a tidal stream with the sails sheeted on the side from which the stream is coming
12 Bringing the boat into the wind
13 Turning the boat away from the wind

Answers on page 79

HEADLINERS

Each of the following vessels has been connected with a memorable incident. Can you say what it is?

1 *Dei Gratia*
2 HMS *Amethyst*
3 *U-20*
4 *Asgard*
5 USS *Missouri*
6 *Merrimack*
7 *Californian*
8 *Birkenhead*
9 *Torrey Canyon*
10 *Altmark*
11 HMS *Rattler*
12 *Turbinia*
13 HMS *Kelly*
14 *Bellerophon*
15 *Ohio*
16 *St Roch*
17 HMS *Camperdown*
18 *Aurora*
19 *America*
20 HMS *Curacoa*
21 USS *Pueblo*
22 HMAS *Melbourne*
23 HMS *Lutine*

Answers on page 80

WE'VE GOT PROBLEMS (5)

Sidney has at last got afloat, or rather he hasn't, since he has just run aground. He has attempted to lay out a kedge anchor with the dinghy but suddenly he finds there is a thumb knot in the warp. He hasn't time to row back and clear it because the tide is falling fast, nor can he free the knot from the anchor end because the two have been spliced together.

How can Sidney quickly clear the knot?

Answer on page 81

IN YOUR JUDGEMENT (6)

A man chartered a boat for a three-month holiday. The contract included a let-out clause saying that if there were a major engine breakdown which laid the boat up for a period of seven days or longer then the contract would be cancelled and the charterer would have the balance of his fee returned. This allowed for the temperamental behaviour of small marine engines although the contract stated that to the best of operator's knowledge the engine was in a good and serviceable condition and no major trouble need be expected. It also said that, provided reasonable notice were given, the operators would see that the batteries were charged and the engine ready to be started.

In the event, this was not done. Although the charterer had given plenty of notice of his arrival, the batteries had not been charged and the engine could not be started. The charterer was furious. He said the contract was cancelled because the operator had broken the agreement. Subsequently, the operator took the man to court.

Can you guess what the outcome was?

Answer on page 81

1

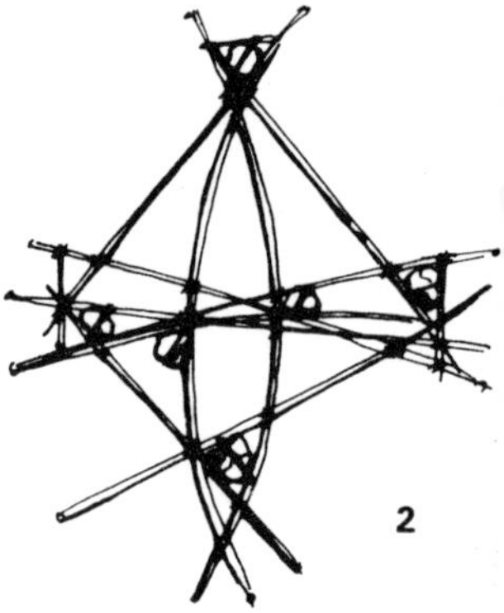

2

3

4

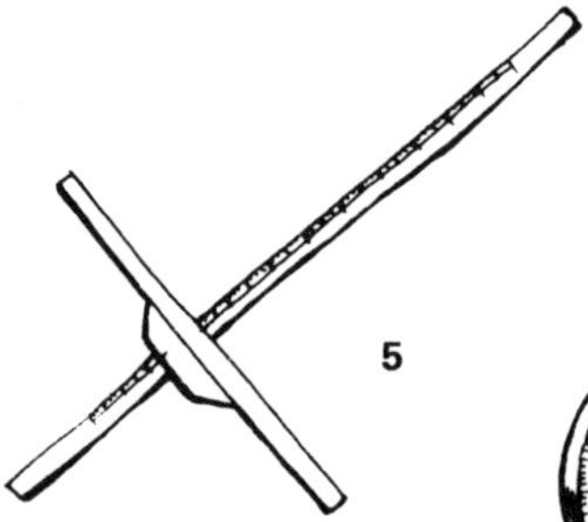

5

6

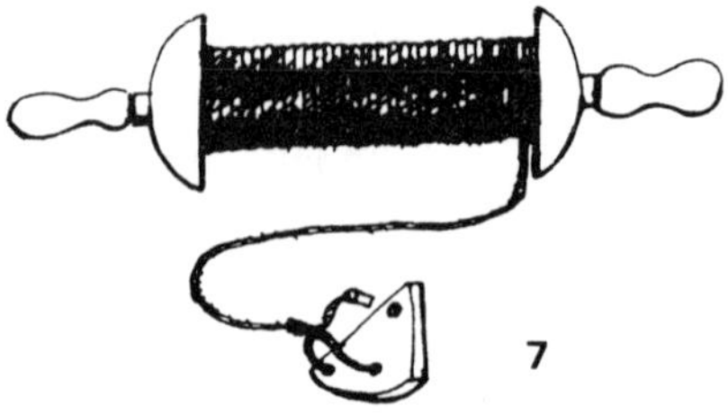

7

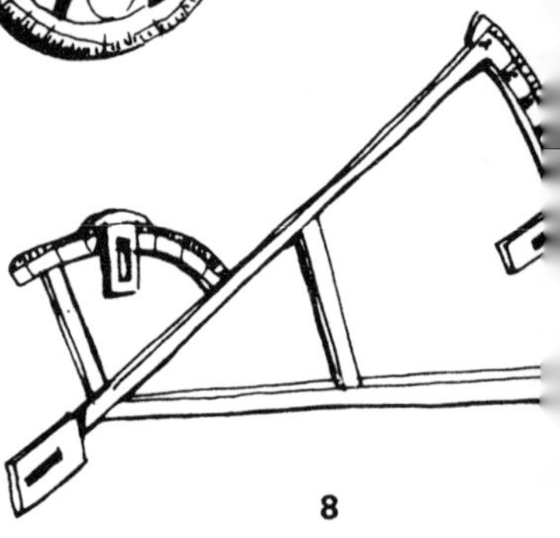

8

WHAT ARE THEY?

Can you name or suggest what these early navigation instruments and devices (*see opposite page*) were used for?

Answers on pages 81-82

SALTY TALK

Do you know, or can you guess, the origins of these popular expressions?

1 Between the devil and the deep blue sea
2 A blind eye
3 Bottle up
4 By and large
5 Chance your arm
6 Close quarters
7 Copper bottom investment
8 Cut and run
9 Cut of his jib
10 Dummy run
11 Hi-jack
12 Horse latitudes
13 Making a rod for your own back
14 No room to swing a cat
15 Over a barrel
16 Put through the hoop
17 Real McCoy
18 Take the gilt off the gingerbread
19 Touch and go
20 Toe the line

Answers on pages 82-83

IN YOUR JUDGEMENT (6)

In November 1947, the skipper of the sailing barge *The Enid* wrote to the harbour master at Neath to advise him of his arrival on the early morning tide on the 11th, requesting that the entrance lights of the river be lit. (In those days oil lamps were used.) The channel was navigable for about four hours either side of HW and all concerned knew that the river was only lit at dark tides on request. The lights involved were the outer Monkstone light, which were, in fact, two lights (an upper and lower) at a distance from each other to form a short transit, plus a few single lights in the river.

The Enid crossed Swansea Bay in the early hours. There was a strong onshore wind, frequent squalls, which reduced visibility and a strong flood tide. She shaped in towards the land on a NE course with the hope of picking up the Monkstone but due to the harbour master's negligence the Monkstone had not been lit. Nor indeed had any of the other approach lights. Unaware of this the crew of the *The Enid* picked up two shore lights which appeared to them to be in the 'right' position and altered course towards the land. They motored for a while but then, with following wind and flooding tide they swept in under bare poles. After a mile they ran aground on the Baglan Sands. The barge was badly damaged and it was several weeks before she could be salvaged. The barge owners claimed against the Neath Harbour Commissioner for a breach of duty.

Did they win their case? Who do you feel was to blame?

Answer on page 84

IDENTIFY A DINGHY (1)

Here are the sail marks of some popular dinghies. How many can you recognise?

(a)

(b)

(c)

(d)

(e)

(f)

(g)

(h)

(i)

(j)

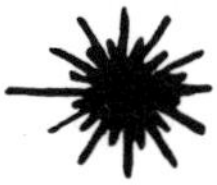
(k)

(l)

(m)

(n)

(o)

(p)

(q)

(r)

(s)

(t)

Answers on page 84

ODD MAN OUT

One of each of the following groups has no business being there. Which one is it?

1 Hoy; coble; lerret; dory; mumble bee; tosher
2 Pampero; levanter; scirocco; mistral; gregale; tramontana
3 Surgeon; constrictor; timber; crown; lover; thumb
4 Warping; drudging; kedging; quanting; ghosting
5 Solent; Tyne; Arun; Watson; Bradford; Oakley
6 Raffee; course; Jimmy Green; royal; spanker; blooper
7 Afterguard; wasters; foretopman; sentinel; libertymen
8 Hipper; Hood; Jean Bart; Nimitz; Tromp; Forrestal; Nelson
9 John Illingworth; Robert Clark; Nat Herreshoff; Colin Archer; Humphrey Barton
10 Strip; cold moulded; splined; clinker; double diagonal; seam-battened; carvel
11 *Sir Thomas Lipton*; *Moxie*; *Pen Duick II*; *Umupro Jardin*; *Club Mediterranée*
12 Sea-cock; strum-box; limbers; bilge; scuppers

Answers on pages 84-85

WE'VE GOT PROBLEMS (6)

Our man was having a quiet cup of tea at anchor when suddenly he heard a shout for help. Some chap in a dinghy calling out, 'How do I get this thing to go forwards?' Sidney saw his problem in a trice – inexperience. The man clearly did not know how to sail. Downwind there were rocks and while he wasn't being swept any nearer, he wasn't increasing the distance from them either; in fact, all he was doing was broad-reaching up and down under Sidney's stern and calling on Sidney to *do something!*

But what could Sidney do? He had tried reaching him with a heaving line but the line was too short. And then when he secured a mooring warp to it to lengthen the scope the thing was too heavy to throw. He did consider letting go the anchor and motoring down to the man, or even veering more cable. But when he checked there was only two feet of water under his stern so any movement was out of the question.

How could Sidney save the man?

Answer on page 85

CROSSWORD (2)

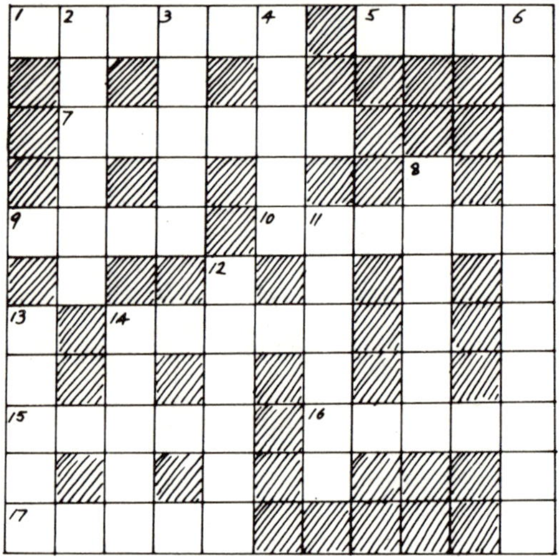

Across

1 Always at Ostar's court (6)

5 Executed British admiral (4)

7 It's a drag (6)

9 Sometimes as untidy as it sounds (4)

10 Worse than its bight? (6)

14 Drawn level (5)

15 An anchorage (5)

16 Edible sea vegetable (5)

17 You can pay with this (5)

Down

2 Reverse currents (6)

3 Moorings on the extreme left (5)

4 This straight line is not the shortest distance (5)

6 Ship's variety cannot be eaten (11)

8 Dangerous for its suddenness (6)

11 Unsuccessful invasion fleet (6)

12 A painful way to lose weight (6)

13 Masefield made it lyrical (5)

14 It's one way to be taken (5)

Answer on page 86

SHIPS OF EXPLORATION AND DISCOVERY

From early times man has used ships to discover the planet, to explore and colonise. Can you name the following?

1 The three ships in which Columbus set out to discover the New World in 1492
2 The ship in which Darwin made his round-the-world voyage
3 The US Navy submarine which successfully navigated beneath the North Pole in 1958
4 The papyrus raft upon which Thor Heyerdhal initially set out to prove that Egyptian navigators could have crossed the Atlantic
5 The two ships under Captain Cook's command in his final expedition of 1772
6 Sir Ernest Shackleton's ship which became fast in the ice causing the crew to take to the boats
7 The ship which, according to legend, carried the Argonauts in search of the Golden Fleece
8 The name of the converted minesweeper which is the base for Jacques Cousteau's underwater explorations
9 thc sewn leather boat named after an Irish monk in which Tim Severin crossed the Atlantic
10 The sloop in which Roald Amundsen sailed to become the first man to navigate the North West Passage
11 Ferdinand Magellan's flagship
12 The British survey ship which, in a remarkable 4-year hydrographic survey between 1872–6, discovered and gave her name to the ocean's deepest hole
13 The 'worn and leaky sloop' in which Matthew Flinders charted South Australia and the Great Barrier Reef
14 The name of the ship which would have been more famous had she not been so leaky that her passengers and crew had to abandon her and sail in the *Mayflower* instead

Answers on page 86

SOMETHING COCK-EYED SOMEWHERE

These were intended to be harbour plans for a yachtsman's guide to the Solent and its surrounds. The trouble is the titles have got lost and the printer, without any guidance, has printed them upside down – or, in some cases – the wrong way round.

Can you sort them out and tell which is which?

Answers on page 86

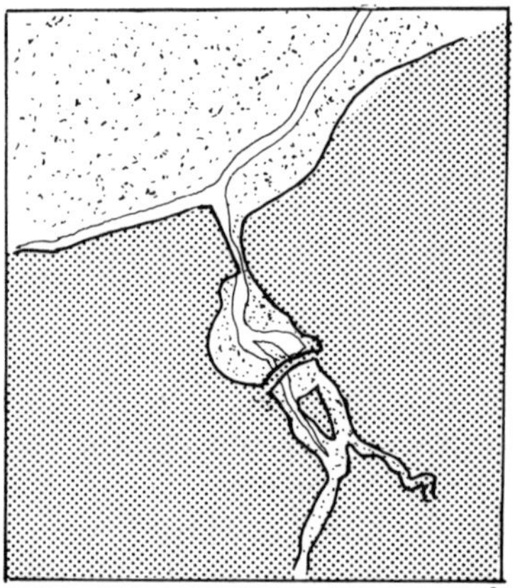

1

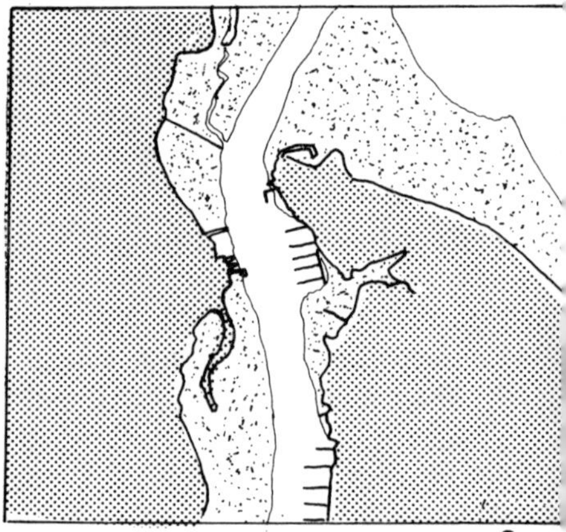

2

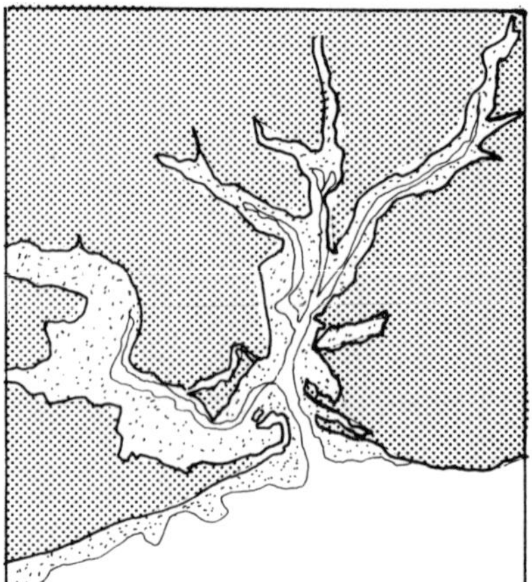

3

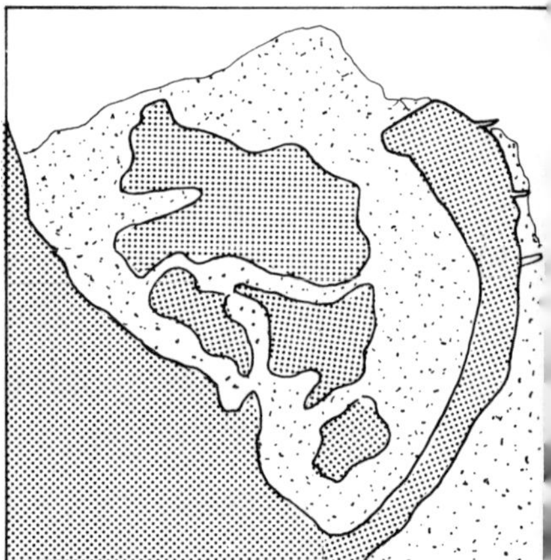

4

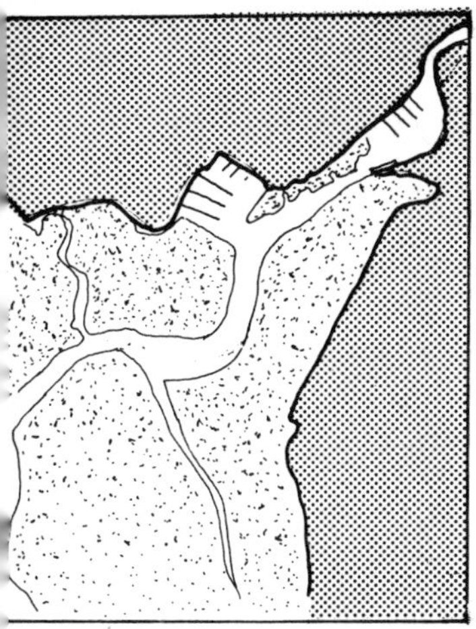

5

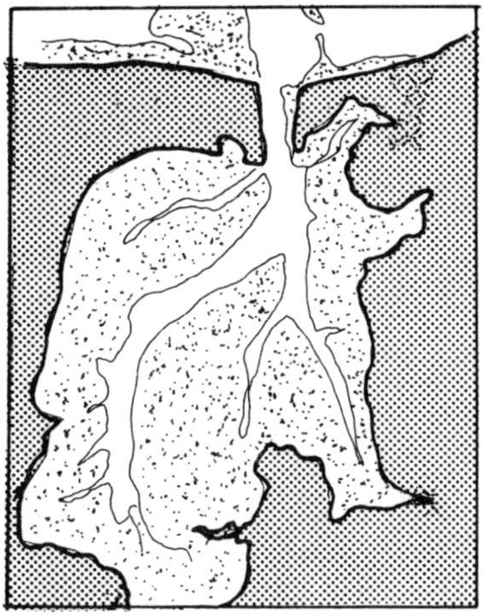

6

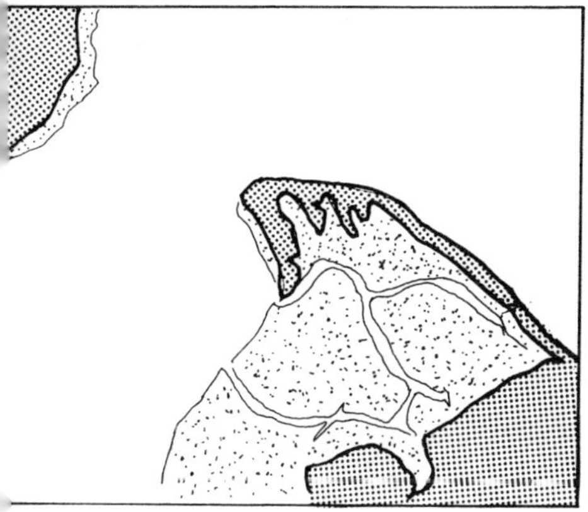

7

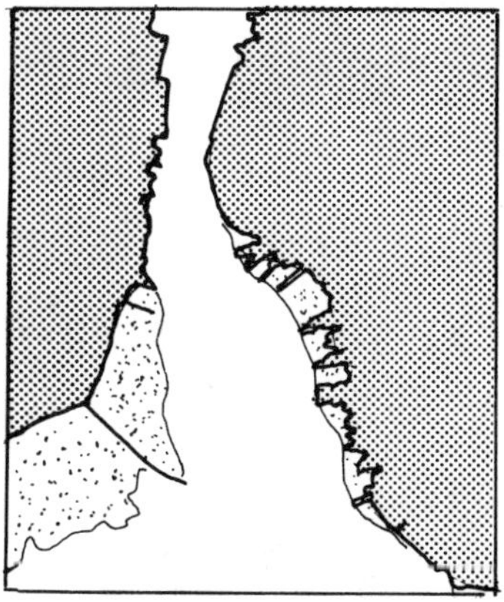

8

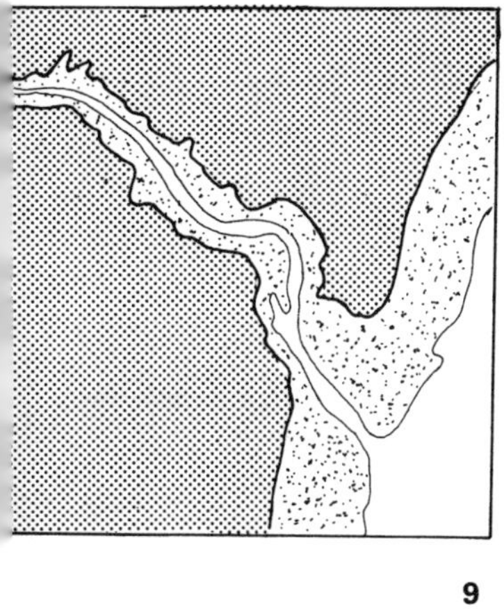

9

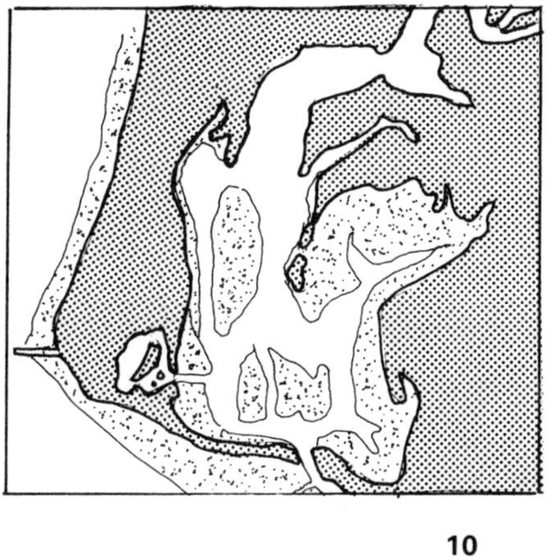

10

WORKING SAIL FROM WHERE?

Here are a dozen well-known working boats from around the world and while not all are now commercially employed, examples of each may still be found.

What are their names, and from where do they come?

1

2

3

4

5

6

7

8

9

10

11

12

Answers on page 87

CROSSWORD (3)

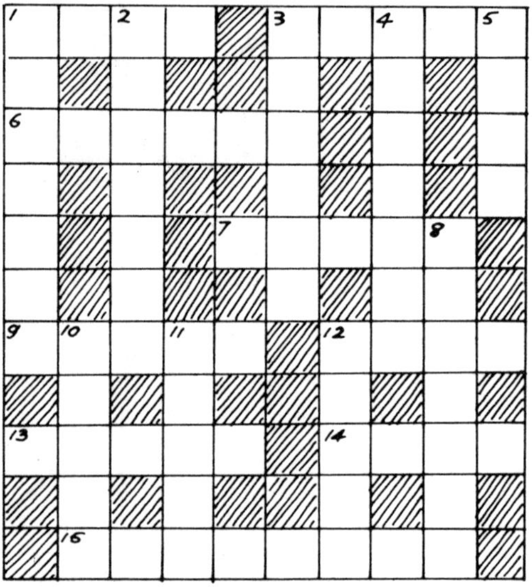

Across

1 Secure in a Hampshire valley (4)

3 It runs around the block (5)

6 Eliminates chafe at the bow (6)

7 Admiral whose name made it sound like a family business (5)

9 Anti-submarine device (5)

12 Something between a skate and a leg (4)

13 Every offshore boat should have one (5)

14 Athwartship movement (4)

15 The Irish pattern are unsightly (8)

Down

1 A telling force (7)

2 The name survives but not the material (7)

3 A monthly rise (6)

4 This type is not seen on canals (7)

5 Baby's boat (4)

8 A sharp lookout is kept at this lighthouse (7)

10 On the lowest level (5)

12 A call of the sea it is best to ignore (5)

Answers on page 87

GUESSTIMATE

Most of us have difficulty remembering facts and figures and when it comes to solving problems we rely on empirical knowledge. We call it 'a common sense approach'. But how safe is this and how close do we come to the scientific answer? Here are a few questions designed to test this popular fancy.

1 You are walking down to the harbour for an afternoon's sail. Your friend, who has invited you to sail in his dinghy, had said that if the wind is 15 knots or above then you won't go out. You look up at the trees, the smaller branches are beginning to move. In the gutter an item of waste paper is lifted and in a skip filled with rubble you notice that dust is rising. Do you continue walking to the harbour, or turn around and go home?

2 You are standing in the cockpit with your head 6 feet above the water. You can see roughly 3 miles. How much farther could you see from the top of a 30-foot mast?

3 You are sunbathing on deck in the altogether. Suddenly your companion shouts in alarm. He says he can see a cross-Channel ferry coming directly towards you! He says the bow wave is visible already. How long have you got to grab a towel?

4 You have been asked by your club to build a raft using 40-gallon oil drums to bring ashore a huge ceremonial cannon now housed in the starting platform. The cannon weighs one ton. Your local garage says he can lend you the oil drums. How many do you need?

5 You have run ashore on a falling tide and the weather is threatening. A fishing boat comes up and offers to pluck you off. The problem is that he cannot get close and is unable to throw you a rope. The only rope you have which is both long enough and light enough to throw is something between the size of a bean-stick and a Panatella (actually 10mm diam) and it is nylon. The fisherman tells you he has a bollard pull of two tons. Do you use the rope, will it hold?

6 Elsewhere in this book there is a drawing of a kedge warp in which an overhand (or thumb) knot has appeared. If you ignored the knot and went ahead and used the rope, what sort of percentage loss of strength might you have to take into account?

7 There is a dangerous rock 100 metres off the end of the harbour breakwater. On the breakwater end you can see men fishing and although your eyesight is normal the features of their faces are not visible but simply a pale blur. Are you far enough from the end of the breakwater to clear the rock?

8 You are feeling your way along in fog navigating from one buoy to another. The distance from Scower buoy to Beer Top buoy is six cables, your boat is doing four knots over the ground. If you passed Scower Buoy at 1018 and at 1030 Beer Top buoy has still not been seen, is it still ahead or have you missed it?

9 A friend has rigged a set of sheer legs to lift the engine out of his boat. The handbook says engine and gearbox together weigh 1,000lbs and your friend is certain that the two of you employing a 4-part tackle should lift this easily. Is he correct?

10 You are interested in buying a 30-foot medium displacement sailing cruiser. You discover she has a 25-lb CQR anchor with a short length of chain and 12mm (diam) nylon warp. The owner insists his ground tackle is ample for the size and displacement of the boat. Do you agree?

Answers on pages 87-88

WE'VE GOT PROBLEMS (7)

Sidney is in real trouble this time, and it isn't his fault! He has picked up a crab line with his propeller and what with the wind and tide the crab line is now bar tight and he cannot begin to clear it. What can he do?

Answer on page 88

SPOT THE LIGHTHOUSE

A lighthouse is a cylindrical stone tower with a lantern on the top – a bare description that gives no hint of the wide variety of styles, colours, shapes, size, features and settings of such principal navigation marks. Despite their design requirement that they should show a light at a considerable height and withstand the weather, no two lighthouses look the same.

Can you name these?

1

2

3

4

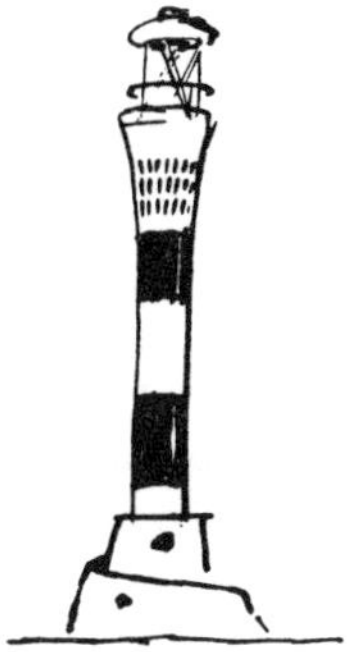

5

6

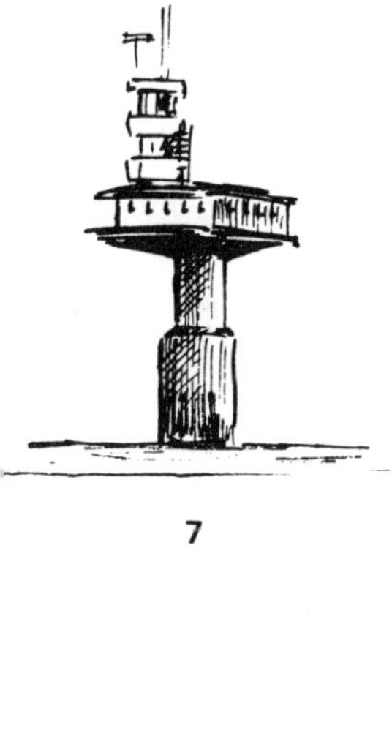

7

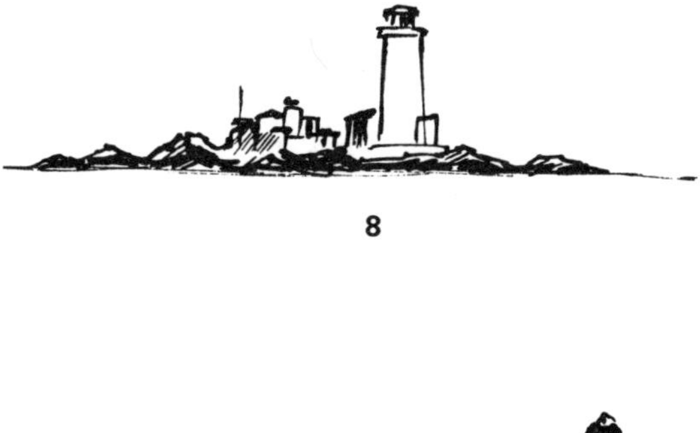

8

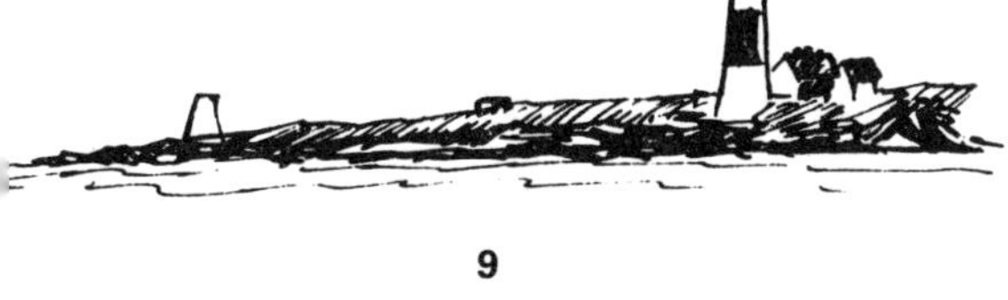

9

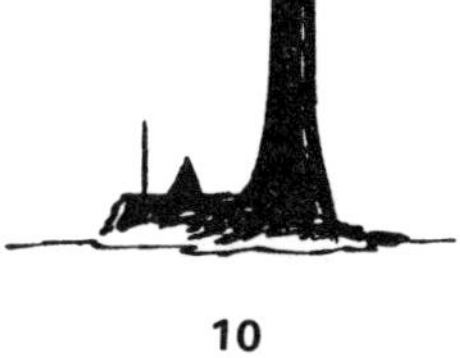

10

Answers on page 89

WATER WISDOM

1 The greatest tides occur in the Bay of Fundy. What is their maximum height?

2 Hurricanes contain tremendous energy. If the energy contained in the average hurricane could be harnessed and transformed into domestic electricity it would provide enough to . . . Can you offer a suitable analogy?

3 Arctic icebergs travel south in the eastern Atlantic. Can you suggest how far south the furthest has travelled?

4 If the northern hemisphere is 60 per cent water, what percentage of water does the southern hemisphere contain?

5 What brand new island arose from the sea near Iceland in 1963?

6 The Mediterranean is poetically blue. But scientifically can it be any more blue than other seas?

7 Can you say within 20 per cent how fast a giant tsunami travels?

8 How deep is the deepest ocean hole in the Pacific?

9 How high was the highest wave ever recorded?

10 Can you suggest within 30 per cent how many thunderstorms occur throughout the world at any given moment of time?

11 What makes the sea salty?

12 The oceans were formed when the earth cooled and the enveloping cloud burst. Scientists believe it then rained non-stop for . . . well, how many years do you think it would need to rain to fill up an estimated 325,000,000 cubic miles of ocean?

13 Atmospheric pressure can raise or lower the height of the sea. Additionally, the slurping effect of tides can raise sea level. If the Pacific Ocean were suddenly frozen on a perfectly still day then what difference might you expect to measure between the humps and depressions?

14 What is the largest inland sea in the world?

15 Satellite measurements have found that the Mediterranean Sea slopes downhill from Cannes to Algiers. Can you guess by how much?

16 Storms beneath the surface of the sea do occur and are much greater than those on the surface. True or false?

17 Six million years ago the Mediterranean was a sunken desert 10,000 feet deep. Then one day the Atlantic burst through and an estimated 10,000 cubic miles of water poured in. It was the greatest waterfall the world has ever known. But for how long do you suppose it continued?

Answers on page 89

IN YOUR JUDGEMENT (7)

A yachtsman on passage from Littlehampton to Bembridge developed a headache and decided to put into the tidal harbour of Pagham and anchor overnight. But Pagham is a nature reserve and a local byelaw prohibits mooring. A warden asked the yachtsman on arrival whether he was in distress and, on receiving a negative reply, asked him to leave directly. This the man refused to do although wind and sea conditions were favourable. Later he appeared before Chichester magistrates who fined him for mooring his boat in a nature reserve without reasonable excuse. He appealed to a higher court insisting he was not 'moored', he was anchored, and asserted there was a public right of way in all tidal waters. Did he win or lose his appeal?

Answer on page 89

IN YOUR JUDGEMENT (8)

A yacht insured for £4500 suffered a total loss by fire. The insurance company alleged overvaluation and said that only a few days before insuring the boat the owner had been prepared to sell the yacht for £2850. They claimed this invalidated the policy and the case went to court. What conclusion do you imagine was reached?

Answer on page 90

DEAR MUM, IT'S A . . . !

Young Johnnie Greenhorn went for a sail in *Sea Cow* and what a nightmare it turned out to be. The boat had so many shortcomings. He tried to describe them in a letter home to his mother but he didn't know the terms.

Can you supply the ones he was looking for?

Dear Mum,

When I saw *Sea Cow* at anchor she didn't look right. She was (**1**) bent upwards like a banana. And she was (**2**) tippy because when I stepped aboard she rolled over so far under my weight that the deck edge went underwater.

We motored out of harbour but it was dangerous because she (**3**) zig-zagged so badly. And the propeller (**4**) made a whirring sound like it was spinning in the air. When we got the sails up the skipper let me steer but it was hard because with every puff she (**5**) flew up in the wind. The skipper said that perhaps if we (**6**) rolled up some of the mainsail it might reduce the (**7**) imbalance.

Then the skipper said let's try her on the other tack but I couldn't get her round. She just hung (**8**) in limbo with her sails all shaking. It was ages before we could get her to (**9**) go off on the other tack. Nor did it help when we did because every time she hit a wave there was a terrific (**10**) banging up under the bow. The skipper came up to say that up in the forward cabin he could actually see the sides (**11**) flexing in and out. He said we should have to (**12**) stop the boat by backwinding the jib and lashing the tiller downwind. but it didn't work very well when we tried it. Apart from the (**13**) fact that we were blown several miles downwind the boat kept (**14**) shooting forward. The skipper said it wasn't helped by too much (**15**) stuff like cockpit dodgers and sprayhoods.

'Only one thing to do!' he shouted 'Run before it.' So we hoisted the jib. Two minutes later she **(16)** spun round out of control and that's why I'm writing this letter in France.

Your loving son,
Johnnie

P.S. The Consul says I'll be coming home DBS whatever that means.

Answers on page 90

YACHTS & YACHTSMEN

Here are some very well known yachts. Can you give the name of the yachtsmen and women principally associated with them?

1 *British Steel*
2 *Gypsy Moth IV*
3 *Pen Duick*
4 *Mischief*
5 *Spray*
6 *Legh II*
7 *Shamrock*
8 *Firecrest*
9 *Jester*
10 *Moonraker*
11 *Wanderer III*
12 *Express Crusader*
13 *Tzu Hang*
14 *Lively Lady*
15 *Myth of Malham*
16 *Perseus*
17 *Joshua*
18 *Islander*
19 *Trekka*
20 *Three Legs of Mann*
21 *Moxie*
22 *Ice Bird*
23 *Endeavour*
24 *Miss England II*
25 *Rose Rambler*

Answers on page 90

CHOICE OF CUT

It is your second day at the sail loft, still no news of the boss and the girl from the exhaust parts. The 'phone rings. It is an irate owner who tells you his sails have still not been delivered. He cannot wait any longer, he has an important race this weekend and will collect the sails personally in a quarter of an hour. Before he slams down the phone you have just time to learn that he has ordered a horizontal cut main, a scotch cut jib and a Hood mitre cut spinnaker.

There are nine new sails on the loft floor, which are the ones he wants?

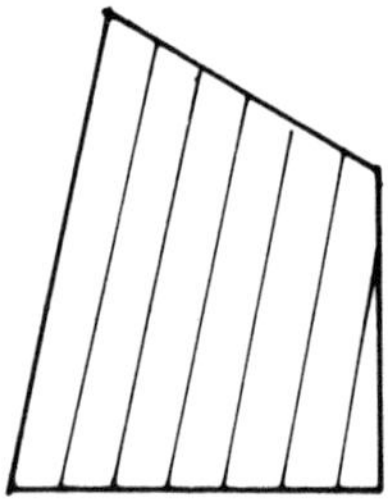

1

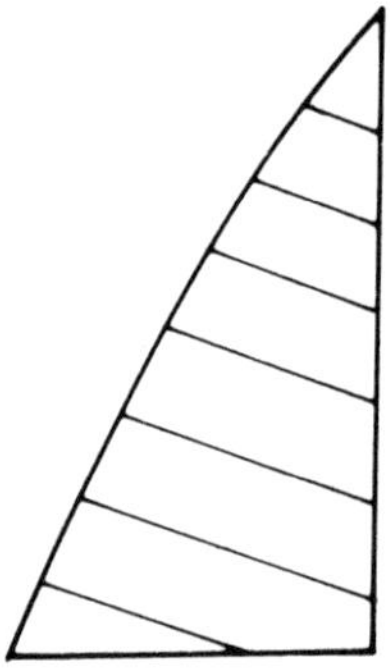

2

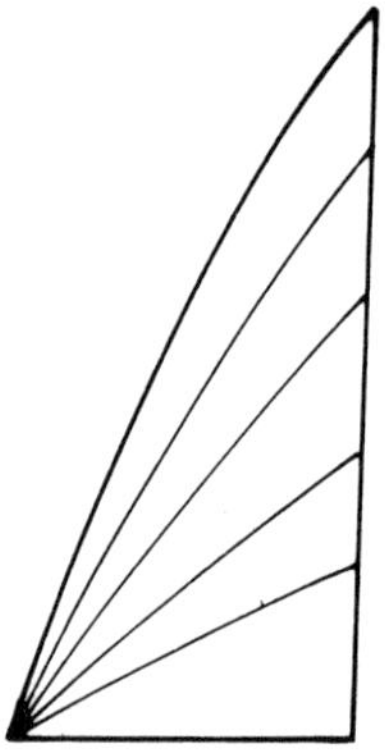

3

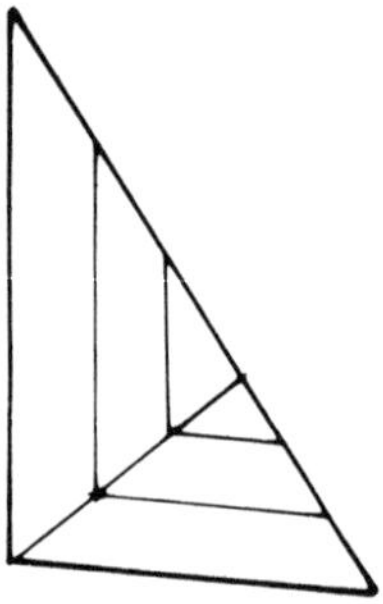

4

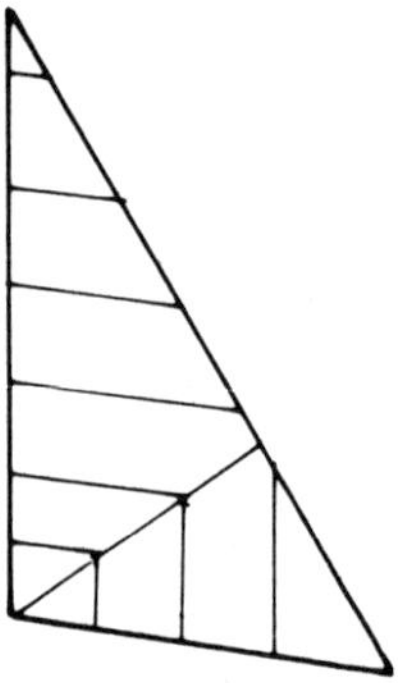

5

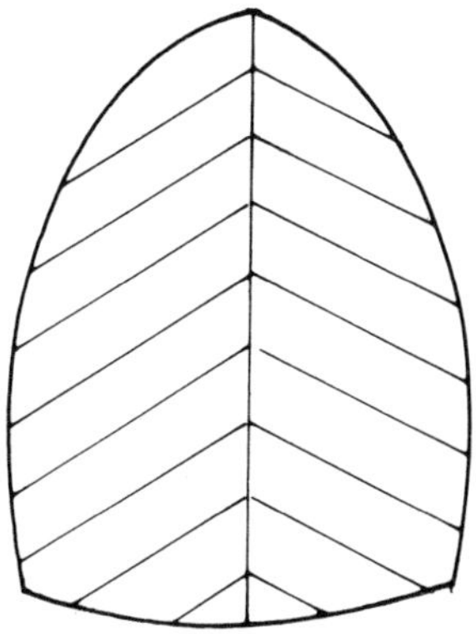

6

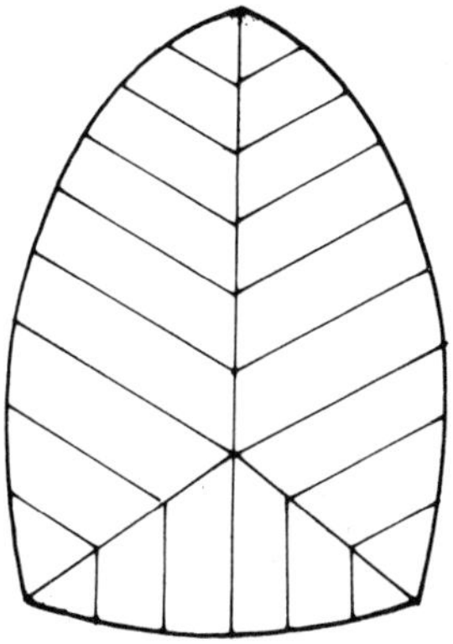

7

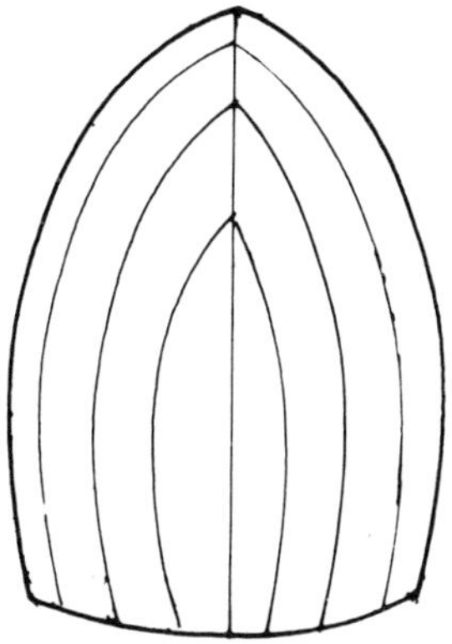

8

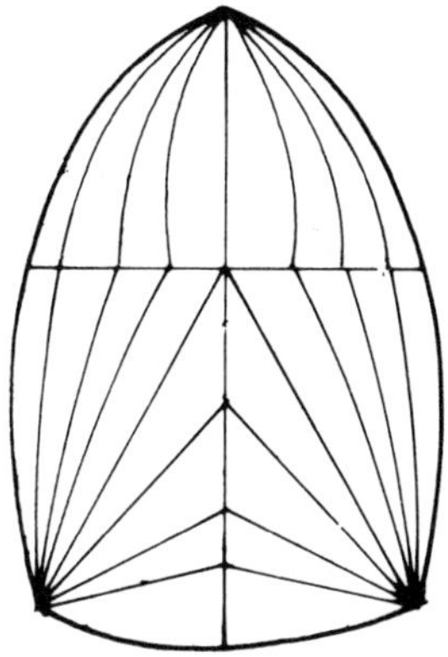

9

Answers on page 90

IN YOUR JUDGEMENT (9)

A 27-foot catamaran was damaged on passage from the West Country to the Channel Islands, in a position some twenty miles out in the Channel. Her owner claimed on his insurance which was a dinghy policy stating that he was protected 'within the United Kingdom whether ashore or afloat'. The insurance company refused the claim insisting that the Channel Islands were not a part of the United Kingdom.

Were they correct and should the claim have been allowed?

Answer on page 91

IDENTIFY A DINGHY (2)

Here are the sail marks of some popular dinghies.
How many can you recognise?

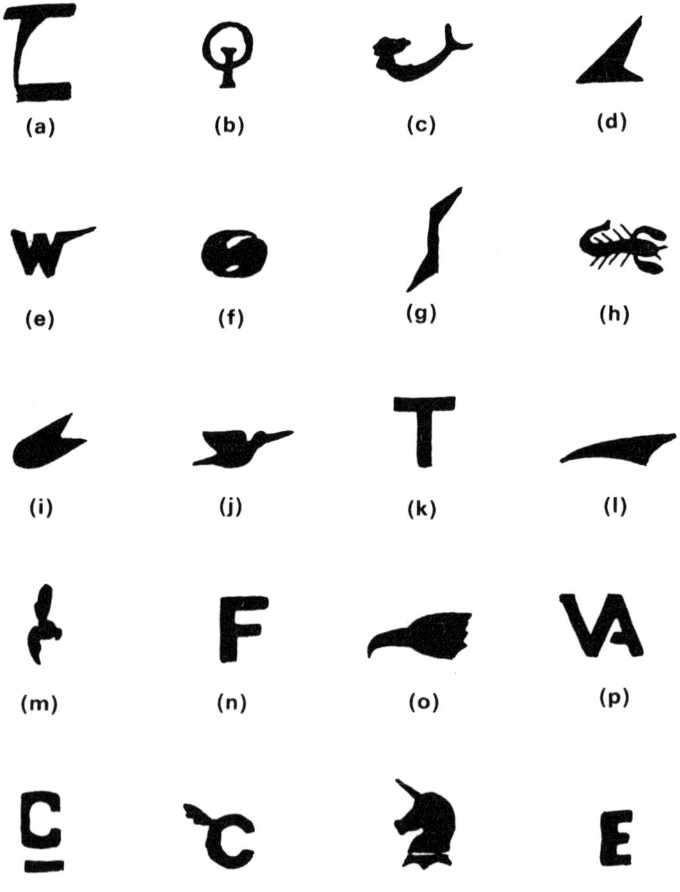

Answers on page 91

WHAT'S WRONG HERE?

How many obvious faults and omissions can you find in this yacht just clearing harbour?

Answers on page 91

FLAG ETIQUETTE

However trivial it may seem today, great importance has always been attached to the business of putting up the bunting. Protocol grew often from the serious matter of identification of an enemy or the importance of battle communication, so getting it right was absolutely vital and ships have been sunk for apparently trivial oversights. Even today, vessels which contravene flag restrictions and laws can risk heavy fines. Here are a few questions designed to test your knowledge of flag drill. Can you say whether these statements are correct or incorrect?

1 A vessel flies its ensign from sunrise to sunset
2 A boat which is racing can wear its ensign at the masthead
3 If you loan your boat to a foreign national he may wear the red ensign.
4 By law every British yacht should carry a red ensign (or designated ensign) whether registered or not
5 If the boat's owner holds a reserve commission and a warrant to wear the blue ensign then this is the ensign which the vessel must hoist whether the owner is sailing in the vessel or not
6 There are occasions when a vessel may wear two or more ensigns
7 When dipping the ensign in salute you should wait for the other vessel to lower her flag before re-hoisting
8 You should salute all foreign warships
9 You should salute all vessels wearing the white ensign and the yacht of the Trinity House Elder Brethren
10 In foreign ports the courtesy flag is hoisted on the starboard side
11 In countries which have both a national and a maritime flag it is national flag which is shown

12 If you wear a blue ensign then officers from Royal Navy ships can demand to see the warrant that gives you this authority

13 There is no precedent in the wearing of club burgees

14 A vessel over 50 tons gross which does not show her ensign when entering or leaving a British port may be fined

15 Small yachts will be excused wearing ensigns while in foreign ports due to the difficulty in showing them

16 At sea it is customary to dip the ensign to any yacht you pass

17 In cases of national mourning every flag aboard the vessel is worn half mast

18 If the owner dies then all flags, ensign, burgee and house flag are half-masted

19 A Royal Naval ship signals both a British yacht and a fishing boat to hoist their colours. If neither comply then only the yacht can be fined

20 Some countries have very properly laid down codes of flag signals, the United States for example. If you carelessly allow the Stars and Stripes to touch the deck you are liable to be fined

Answers on page 92

WHO ARE THEY?

Here are potted biographies of some well-known nautical personalities. Only their names have been omitted. Who are they?

1 The mutineer whose life was spared because he was an invaluable pilot. He survived the circumnavigation after his leader perished and was decorated by the King of Spain
2 Erstwhile scoutmaster who landed in trouble with his seniors for taking his troop cross-Channel and up to Paris in a whaler. Close friend of the Royals, notoriously profane
3 An American sailor, an enlisted man and pioneer vegetarian. Sweetheart Olive
4 Marine painter and war artist who devised the method of dazzle-painting ships in World War I and was responsible for all camouflage in World War II
5 Australian sailor, author and nautical researcher who bought a four-masted barque which he renamed the *Joseph Conrad* and sailed her around the world with a crew of youngsters. Later went on to command landing craft, sailed a Tudor warship to America, was master of the Outward Bound School. He also sailed with and wrote about the Portuguese Grand Banks fishing fleet and Arab dhows
6 Designer who came to prominence in the 1930s for his successful ocean racer *Dorade*. This embodied many novel features which were generally adopted for offshore racers. He was co-designer and crewed in several America's Cup defenders. Also helped design 21,000 DUKWs
7 Admiral of the Blue, scourge of the Barbary pirates, was shipwrecked but swept safely ashore on account of his enormous bulk which kept him afloat. Murdered by a woman for the blue emerald ring he wore
8 Fought the British with a primitive stone-slinging gun but later attended HMS *Worcester* as a cadet and referred to England as his second mother country. Defeated a numerically superior enemy which had sailed half way around the world to do battle

9 French channel swimmer and doctor who crossed the Atlantic in a raft named *L'Hérétique* to prove that survivors can live principally on what the sea provides

10 Englishman who had his first yacht built in Riga, married Trotsky's secretary, wrote a book about Oscar Wilde and was sued, and was overseas correspondent for the *Manchester Guardian*. Despite his presumed love of children his autobiography has no reference to his own child

11 Scottish-born sailor who became a folk hero in America, an admiral in the Russian navy, and was given a state funeral in France

12 French airman and tennis champion. While being presented with the Légion d'Honneur aboard a destroyer in recognition of his yachting achievements he noticed that his yacht, which was being towed by the ship, had been pulled under and sunk. A humanitarian, he developed an intense concern for Pacific island natives. Attempted to sail home to rejoin French armed services but died in Bora Bora just hours before the Japanese invasion. Unusually, he had named his yacht after himself

13 Dutch seaman immortalised by German composer after an incident while commanding a ship bound for Rotterdam from Batavia

14 British admiral, Governor of New Zealand, shipmate of Charles Darwin. A distinguished surveyor and responsible also for the introduction of examinations for Merchant Navy masters and mates, for synoptic charts and storm cones both of which he invented

15 Consumptive girl who lived with her family on an island and who became publicly acclaimed for her rescue attempt in a coble

Answers on page 92

WE'VE GOT PROBLEMS (8)

It is the last straw for Sidney. Just as he thought the ordeal was over, just as he got his bow and stern lines ashore, made them fast and turned off the engine, a sudden squall came down and blew him clear off the quay and right in the path of a big ship (something which he hasn't seen yet!) How can he quickly get the boat alongside?

Answer on page 93

CROSSWORD (4)

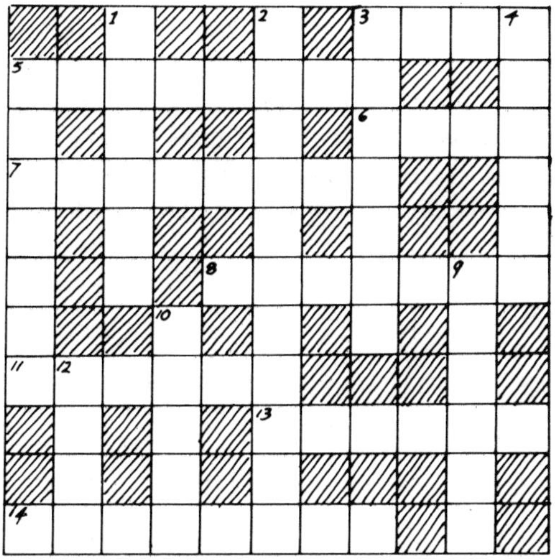

Across

3 Polite term for belly (4)
5 A clean bill (8)
6 Baltic sea port (4)
7 A boat of hope (8)
8 Nailed to the mast (7)
11 Strength member and place for bums (6)
13 These lines are best seen apart (6)
14 The sea is his business (8)

Down

1 A ticket is required (6)
2 Big in the heavens (11)
3 South coast yard (7)
4 Keeps rolling along (6)
5 One flag the navies never use (7)
9 Set above all the rest (6)
10 In North America these might be built with logs (5)
12 Summers in the North Atlantic, sometimes felt but never seen (4)

Answers on page 93

ANIMAL CONNECTIONS

All Noah's animals may have come ashore safely but they certainly left their mark afloat. How many items of apparel, shipboard tasks, or parts of a ship – or indeed types of vessel – can you name with animal connections? You should manage at least twenty.

Answers on pages 94-95

ANSWERS

NAMESAKES

1 Robinson Crusoe
2 Matthew Walker
3 America's Cup
4 A lifejacket and a spinnaker
5 The Kaiser Wilhelm (Kiel) Canal
6 Magellan
7 Major Bill Tilman
8 Mess tin
9 A main boom in 'J' class yachts
10 Dr Hunter
11 Sir Alec Rose
12 Admiral Vernon (known as 'Old Grog' because of the grogram trousers he wore. Sailors called rum issue 'grog' after he ruled that it had to be diluted with water)
13 A sail carried beneath the bowsprit
14 Shanghai
15 The Humboldt
16 An underwater valley north of Alderney
17 Lord Kelvin (soft iron spheres) and Matthew Flinders (bar)
18 'Taffrail' (Captain H. Taprell Dorling)
19 Peter Simple
20 St Elmo (probably a corruption of St Erasmus)
21 Briggs Cunningham
22 Samuel Langhorn Clemens (Mark Twain)
23 Samuel Plimsoll
24 John Smeaton
25 Sir John Wallop
26 Paul Jones

SPOT THE PLOT

1 *The Admirable Crichton* by J. M. Barrie
2 *The African Queen* by C. S. Forester
3 *Typhoon* by Joseph Conrad
4 *The Coot Club* by Arthur Ransome
5 *The Old Man and the Sea* by Ernest Hemingway

IN YOUR JUDGEMENT (1)

Not one of the barge's arguments were accepted. There is a judicial dictum stretching back to medieval times (when this sort of thing was far more prevalent than it is today) that any vessel whose anchor may hazard other vessels must give warning of its presence with a buoy or similar. This the barge had failed to do and the court therefore held them responsible for the damage.

POWER TO HAND

a	Nil	**e**	7:1	**i**	4:1
b	2:1	**f**	4:1	**j**	3:1
c	2:1	**g**	2:1	**k**	2:1
d	3:1	**h**	3:1	**l**	3:1

WHERE DOES SHE COME FROM?

Scotland		*Wales*		*Ireland*		*England*	
AA	Alloa	AB	Aberystwyth	B	Belfast	BK	Berwick-on-Tweed
CL	Carlisle	CF	Cardiff	C	Cork	E	Exeter
DS	Dumfries	CO	Carnavon	D	Dublin	FY	Fowey
FR	Fraserburgh	LA	Llanelli	G	Galway	GY	Grimsby
GW	Glasgow	MH	Milford Haven	WD	Wexford	MN	Maldon
INS	Inverness	SA	Swansea	Y	Youghal	SSS	South Shields

SMOKE TRAIL

The smoke from her funnel is a representation of the apparent wind. It is the resultant of a parallelogram of forces which includes the ship's speed and the strength and direction of the true wind. To resolve this parallelogram draw a line equal to ten units representing the ship's speed. From the outer end of this line draw a second line to the tail end of the smoke. This second line is the true wind which will be found to measure six units and have an angle of 45 degrees from the vertical. This means the true wind is SE and blowing 6 knots.

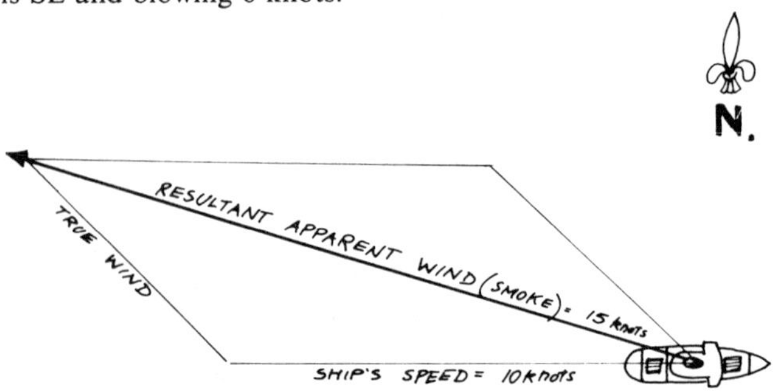

DO YOU REMEMBER WHEN... ? (1)

1 1979
2 1969
3 1977
4 1967
5 1982
6 1968
7 1983

DO YOU REMEMBER WHEN... ? (2)

1 1974
2 1980
3 1972
4 1978
5 1975
6 1971
7 1973

SAY THAT AGAIN

1 Seacock
2 Mattress
3 Tabernacle
4 Boom claw
5 'Ready about!'
6 Whisker pole

WE'VE GOT PROBLEMS (1)

Hardwood wedges are the answer. A new keel block placed on a solid piece of timber to spread the load and the boat can be easily lifted by the systematic use of wedges. They should be driven under each of the after keel blocks and great attention paid to the shores which will loosen as the boat is lifted.

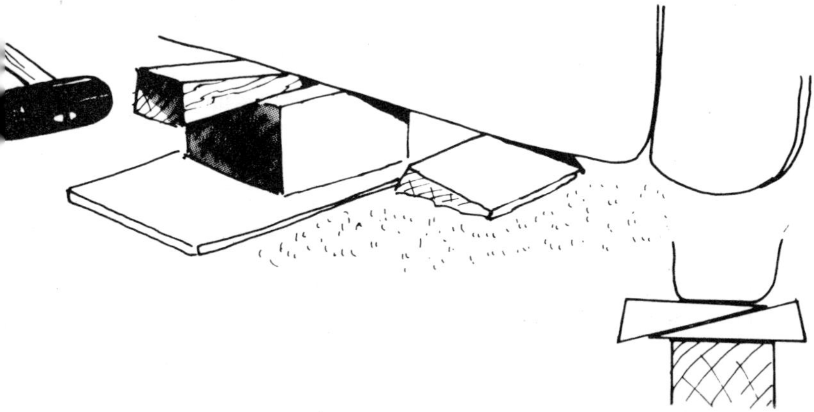

CROSSWORD (1)

1 D				2 F		3 P	O	4 S	H	
5 A	N	6 V	I	L				O		7 S
V		I		8 O	A	9 R		10 S	E	T
I		O		O		A				E
11 T	12 A	L	13 U	R	I	T		14 A	Y	E
15 S	L	A	B			S		W		R
	D		O				16 W	A	S	A
	I		A					S		G
	17 S	A	T	N	A	V		H		E

SILHOUETTES

- **a** *Queen Mary*
- **b** *Great Eastern*
- **c** *Savannah* (first nuclear-powered commercial ship)
- **d** *Titanic*
- **e** *Preussen*
- **f** HMS *Dreadnought*
- **g** *America*
- **h** *Thomas W Lawson*
- **i** HMS *Victory*
- **j** *Yamato* (largest battleship ever built)

NAUTICAL ACRONYMS

1. Twin Screw Diesel Yacht
2. Lighter Aboard Ship
3. Multihull Cruising Racing Association
4. Chosen simply because the letters make the same sound as 'secure' (anchor)
5. Mean Low Water Neaps
6. Yacht Brokers, Designers and Surveyors' Association
7. Very Large Crude Carrier
8. Royal Naval Sailing Association
9. Barge Aboard Catamaran
10. Royal Ocean Racing Club
11. Search and Rescue
12. Roll-on/roll-off (ferry or car transporter)
13. Large Automatic Buoy
14. Royal Naval Reserve
15. International Yacht Racing Union
16. International Maritime Organisation
17. Ship's Inertial Navigation System
18. Royal Fleet Auxiliary
19. Air Cushion Vehicle (hovercraft)
20. Observer Single-handed Transatlantic Race

IN YOUR JUDGEMENT (2)

The case went to the House of Lords who decided that the owner was not liable because he had plainly stated to all concerned that he was abandoning the vessel and was therefore no longer the owner when the expenses were incurred. His case was only successful, however, because (a) there was no evidence of negligence – an owner cannot allow his vessel to sink through decay and then gaily say he is abandoning her – and (b) because there was no Private Act in this harbour, as there sometimes is, which defines owner to mean owner at the time of the sinking, stranding or abandonment of a vessel.

WHOSE ARE THEY?

1 Gaff cutter – main, topsail, staysail and jib (or inner foresail and outer foresail)
2 Ketch or yawl – main, mizzen, working jib and mizzen staysail
3 Staysail schooner – mizzen, upper staysail, lower staysail (or main staysail); foresail and jib
4 Topmast schooner – gaff mizzen and topsail; mainsail, course, royal, raffee, inner jib, outer jib, flying jib

WE'VE GOT PROBLEMS (2)

With the housebrick under one wheel, swing the trailer around its radius. Some upward movement will be gained. Then place the brick under the other wheel and alternate the process.

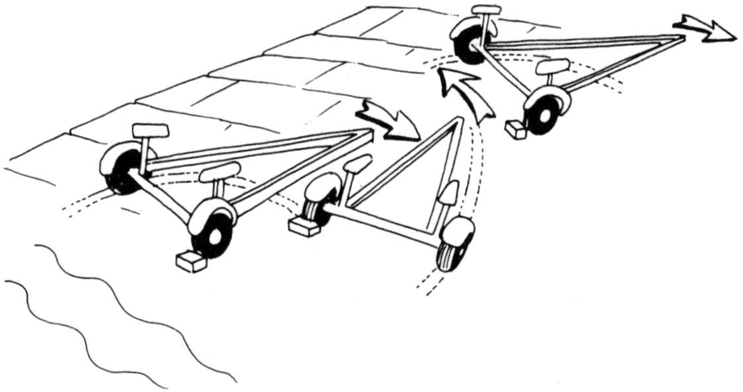

IN YOUR JUDGEMENT (3)

For a salvage claim to be upheld it must be shown that the salved vessel was in a position of danger or that the salvors themselves were exposed to risks in attempting the salvage. Since there were no personal or material risks in this case, judgement depended on whether the yacht was in danger. The court upheld the owner's claim that the repairs could have been carried out by the engineer with the tools on board. The question then was could she have safely anchored? The *Channel Pilot* consulted made no mention of poor holding ground nor was it found that the tides ran anything but true.

Expert opinion said that while there may have been a slight set towards the west this would not be enough to cause substantial damage. The tide was rising which lessened the danger of serious grounding and that any anchoring attempt would have probably have been quite successful. But as indicative as any physical consideration was the behaviour of those present, a factor mentioned by the judge who said that if they believed they were in imminent danger then why did they not anchor immediately. The pilot and skipper went below to consult with the owner and this coupled with the fact that the owner remained in his cabin 'spoke volumes' for their assessment of the danger, said the judge.

The salvage claim was thrown out, although the plaintiffs were entitled to something for the work they had done.

ODDBALLS

1 Montaque whaler
2 The Bessemer ship
3 *Tilikum*
4 Trireme
5 *Surcouf*
6 Grand Banks dory
7 *The Connector*
8 *Planesail* (or more latterly Jacques Cousteau's *Pequod*)
9 *Pen Duick VI*
10 *Thomas W Lawson*
11 *Half-Safe*
12 *Club Mediterranée*
13 *Lividia*
14 *Ocean Bird*
15 Proa
16 The 'Kil' class anti-submarine ships of WW1
17 *Ernest Bazin*

SPOT THE STRUCTURES

a Red Sands Fort
b Spit Sand Fort
c Knock John Gun Tower
d Old Gunfleet Lighthouse
e Nab Tower
f St Helen's Fort
g Girdler Triangular Beacon
h Sunk Gun Tower

WE'VE GOT PROBLEMS (3)

Let the tide do the work. All Sidney needs to find is a heavy baulk of timber to act as a strongback with which to straddle the boat, plus a length of expendable rope and a good sharp knife. As the tide rises, he can position the workboat over the weight and lash it beneath with several turns of rope. Then he must adjust the lashing and position of the strongback as the tide continues to rise until the weight lifts clear; then finally motor the weight out to the mooring space. His sharp knife will cut through the lashings after the chain has been dropped.

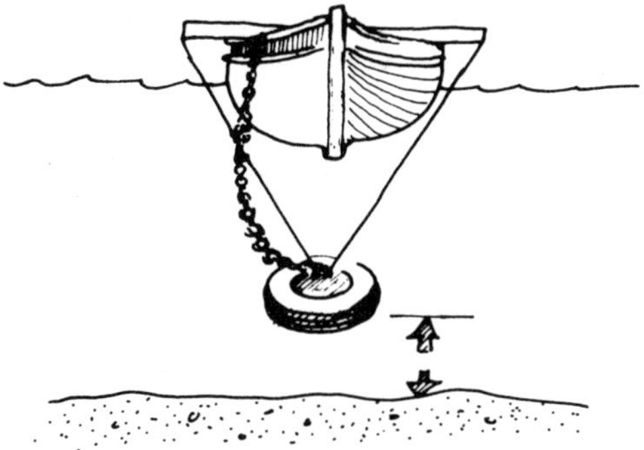

SINGLE-HANDING CAN GET YOU THAT WAY

1 Sir Francis Chichester
2 Margaret Hicks
3 Chay Blyth
4 Fred Rebell
5 Dame Naomi James
6 Donald Crowhurst
7 Bernard Moitessier
8 Paul Rodgers
9 Tristan Jones
10 Colin Irwin
11 Leslie Powles
12 David Cowper
13 Capt William Andrews

COLOURFUL, BUT WHAT DO THEY MEAN?

1 Literally, the ship's bow wave with the inference that it can be clearly seen and therefore the vessel is making good speed
2 The excitement aboard ship and felt by the crew as the ship comes up Channel and home
3 Poorly equipped. From the days when a local parish would send boys to sea and provide them with the minimum of gear
4 A galley chimney but particularly those shaped like an 'H'

5 The barge which collects ships' garbage, or those used by municipal authorities to dump sewage at sea
6 Sailor's name for heaven. A place full of free beer and chorus girls with easy morals
7 A free wind which requires no tacking or difficult sail adjustment. A wind which will take a vessel from one place to another without requiring any nautical skills
8 A mark on the compass bowl which represents the fore and aft line
9 Reciting each point of the compass
10 The job of putting tallow into the recess of the bottom of the hand lead to ascertain the nature of the seabed
11 A light tackle, usually a double and single block giving a 3:1 purchase
12 Sailor's term for stormy petrels and believed to be the harbinger of a storm
13 A flat calm
14 A coloured yarn within a rope to indicate its place of manufacture. Latterly used as a 'Trade Mark' or purpose indicator

ROPE TRICKS

a Swigging
b Frapping
c Bowsing
d Choking (the luff)
e Tailing
f Cheesing
g Mousing
h Marling
i Parbuckling
j Seizing

JUMBLE!

a Boom gooseneck
b Pelican hook
c Highfield lever
d Gudgeon pin
e Mast band
f Forelock (locks stock of Fisherman's anchor)
g Inglefield clip
h Piston type sail hank
i Thimble
j Sail hook (for sewing)
k Boom claws
l Bulldog grip
m Tubular jam cleat
n Shaft anode
o Rope stopper
p Spinnaker pole stowage
q Spinnaker pole end
r Deadeye
s Trapeze handle
t Self-bailer
u Shackle spanner
v Leadline weight
w Oil lamp smoke shade
x Mooring cable swivel
y Deck light

FIRSTS!

1 *Niobe*
2 *Manhattan*
3 *Acadia*
4 USS *Nautilus*
5 *Turbinia*
6 *Nyria*
7 *Atalanta*
8 *Castillia*
9 *Savannah*
10 *Charlotte Dundas*
11 HMS *Dreadnought*
12 *Eilat*
13 USS *Pueblo*
14 *Sirius*
15 *Original*

IN YOUR JUDGEMENT (4)

At the initial court hearing it was held that the shipyard was responsible for the damage but then the case was taken to a Court of Appeal and the decision was overturned. The Lords found that, since it was dangerous to reverse the launch process, the builders had rightly taken the lesser of the two risks. They thought the skipper unreasonable in refusing to move.

SAILING INTO LITERATURE

1 *Dulcibella*
2 *Nautilus*
3 *Pequod*
4 *Pilgrim* and *Alert*
5 *Racundra*
6 *Vital Spark*
7 HMS *Pinafore*
8 HMS *Compass Rose*
9 *Hispaniola*
10 HMS *Ulysses*
11 *Ziethen*
12 *Black Pig*

THERE IS A WORD FOR IT

1 Chinese gybe
2 Taken aback
3 In irons, or in stays
4 Scandalise
5 Backing
6 Let fly
7 Goose-wing, or wing a'wing
8 Sailing full and by
9 Backwinding
10 Over-pressed, or over-canvassed
11 Lee bowing
12 Luff up
13 Pay off, or bear away

HEADLINERS

1 The brigantine which discovered the *Mary Celeste*
2 The sloop which, in 1949, made a dash for freedom down the Yangtse river after being held by communist Chinese
3 The German submarine which sank the *Lusitania* in 1915 and swayed American public opinion against Germany in World War I
4 Erskine Childers' yacht in which he was involved in gun-running for the IRA
5 The battleship in which General MacArthur accepted the Japanese surrender in 1945
6 The Confederate ironclad which duelled with the Union's armoured ship *Monitor*
7 The ship criticised for not coming to the aid of the *Titanic*
8 The troopship whose sinking was ennobled by the discipline and calm of the soldiers who stood in ranks until the seas swept their feet
9 The tanker which ran onto the Seven Stones in 1967 and whose cargo badly polluted British and French beaches
10 The German prison ship successfully stormed by the British destroyer *Cossack* in a Norwegian fjord in 1940
11 The screw-driven sloop which beat the paddle sloop *Alecto* in a tug of war and so established the supremacy of the propeller
12 The steam turbine yacht which stole the show at Queen Victoria's Jubilee when she raced through the Fleet review at 30 knots
13 Lord Louis Mountbatten's ship sunk off Crete in 1942 and immortalised in Noel Coward's film 'In Which We Serve'
14 The sailing warship upon which Napoleon surrendered in 1815
15 The oil tanker which, sinking and lashed to destroyers, brought the vital oil supply to a besieged Malta in 1942
16 The Royal Canadian Mounted Police gaff schooner which navigated the North West Passage in both directions
17 The Mediterranean Fleet flagship which collided and sank the *Victoria* after a signalling error
18 The cruiser preserved in Leningrad aboard which a mutiny helped spark off the 1917 Russian revolution
19 The schooner which won the cup presented to the winner of the Round the Island race in 1851 and which has ever after been known as the America's Cup
20 The light cruiser rammed and sunk by the *Queen Mary* in 1942
21 The US Navy spy ship captured by North Korean gunboats in 1968
22 The Australian aircraft carrier which sank two destroyers: HMAS *Voyager* in February 1964 and, four months later, the US destroyer *Frank E. Evans*
23 The Royal Navy ship sunk with much treasure off the Dutch coast. Her bell was salvaged and hangs in Lloyd's where it is rung whenever there is a disaster

WE'VE GOT PROBLEMS (5)

Enlarge the knot so that it is big enough to pass the dinghy, the anchor and his whole self through it.

IN YOUR JUDGEMENT (6)

The court found the operator at fault for failing to have the batteries charged but considered it a relatively minor problem which could easily have been resolved. If the boat had been found unseaworthy then the charterer could have justifiably cancelled the contract but not for any such small oversight.
'One has to look at the magnitude of the repair and the time required,' commented the judge. 'The yacht would have been substantially available for the period contracted for.'

The charterer could not repudiate the contract and had to pay the balance of his charter fee.

WHAT ARE THEY?

1 Relief charts used by eskimoes. Carved from wood or bone, they indicated the topography of the coastline
2 Polynesian maps. Made from sticks and stones they showed not only the position of islands relative to each other, but also the wave patterns associated with the islands which helped in their detection
3 Primitive compass in which a length of lodestone was made to float in liquid, in this case a barrel of water
4 Traverse board. Used to calculate a ship's course made good over the day. The direction and duration of each new heading was 'pegged' on the board, at the end of the day the 'pegs' were added up and the mean direction found

5 Cross staff. Used for measuring the altitude of the sun. The instrument was put to the eye and the cross bar slid until its upper edge was in line with the sun and its lower edge touched the horizon. A reading from the scale was then taken and the altitude found from table inspection

6 Astrolabe. Used for measuring the altitude of the sun or a star. It was suspended from a thread, the alidade turned about its axis until the sun or star could be sighted along it, and the altitude then read directly from the ring engraved on the scale.

7 The chip log used for measuring the ship's speed. The line was divided and knotted in lengths of 24 feet 5 inches – which is proportionate to the nautical mile as 15 seconds (the graduation of the sand glass) is proportionate to the hour. The line was run out, the sand glass started and the number of knots which passed through the hand in the allotted time was the speed. The 'chip' anchored the line in the water. To haul in, a sharp tug was needed to pull out the bung and collapse it

8 Back staff. This replaced the cross staff and was called such because the observer used it with his back to the sun

SALTY TALK

1 The devil was the most difficult seam in the planking to caulk and, while there is some dispute, it is generally thought to have been the outside one around the deck. A man caulking (or paying) the devil was in danger of being swept into the scuppers by a wave and then washed overboard. Hence the danger implied by the expression

2 From the Battle of Copenhagen, when Nelson put the telescope to his blind eye so that he could claim with honesty that he had not seen the signal telling him to break off the action

3 From the custom of sailors bottling or saving up their daily tot of rum

4 During a ship's passage, on the bad days when there were head winds the ship had to be sailed *by* the wind, and on the good days of free winds the *large* square sails could be set

5 Behaving in a manner which was likely to prejudice rank and pay. Literally to risk losing the good conduct stripes worn on the left arm

6 These were the names given to barricades of timber which were erected around a ship's quarters from which armed raiders – especially privateers – could be repulsed

7 A sound investment, which alludes to the significant advance in ship safety and seaworthiness provided by sheathing the bottom in copper to deter shipworm

8 A quick getaway, literally cutting through the anchor rope (or the sail ties) and running off before the wind

9 A recognition. French and Spanish ships were claimed to have higher cut jibs and by this they could be identified from a distance

10 Torpedo schools used dummy warheads for practice runs

11 Hi-jack was the harlot's call to the sailor. A quick embrace was frequently followed by a bump on the head from a lead-filled handbag and the sailor would find himself waking up in a ship in desperate need of a crew

12 Two derivations; the latitudes were so called because it was here that the crew would make an effigy of a horse and hoist it into the rigging to signify the first month at sea (for which pay had been advanced before sailing); the so-called 'dead horse' month was at an end. Or, because a feature of these latitudes are calm winds and no rains and if the ship made little progress then her water supply would be used up and the horses might have to be slaughtered

13 In the Royal Navy, men awaiting punishment were often required to make their own cat-o'-nine-tails or lash

14 This could refer to the cat-o'-nine-tails and the fact there was no room to brandish it (punishments were mostly carried out on deck). Or, it could allude to the small space required by a cat, which was a small collier, to swing at anchor

15 From the Royal Navy practice of securing a man over the barrel of a cannon in order to carry out a flogging

16 Hammocks had to be rolled tight so they could be used on upper decks as protection against musket fire and splinters. To ensure that they were tight, rolled hammocks were regularly checked by passing them through a hoop. If the hammock did not fit, its owner could expect to be punished

17 From the time of the American prohibition. Bill McCoy was a Canadian boatbuilder with high and very individual morals. Although he ran liquor through the blockade, he never strayed into American territorial waters and he never sold a bottle which was not 100 per cent pure. At a time of much adulterated liquor this was a rare claim and one for which he has been immortalised

18 Gingerbread became the name for the ornate and very vulnerable gilded scrollwork which decorated ships' sterns. A few scuff marks could easily ruin its appearance

19 From a sailing barges' progress upriver. She tacks into the shallows until her leeboard *touches*, then promptly puts her helm down to *go* about

20 Method of making a stability curve for a sailing ship using the crew as movable ballast. Chalk lines were drawn at intervals down the deck. To make the ship heel (and thereby measure the angle), the crew would advance forward and stand with the toes on each line

IN YOUR JUDGEMENT (6)

The Court found that while there was a clear case of a breach of duty on the part of the Harbour Commissioners for failing to light the Monkstone, the question was, did this fully explain the accident? They criticised the barge skipper for not steering exact compass courses and for attempting to home on a single light when the strong wind and flooding tide were all the while setting him to the east. Had he taken cross checks and bearings he would have realised this. They also questioned the wisdom of making firm decisions on any fixed light and steering remorselessly towards it when squally showers could obliterate adjacent channel lights that might otherwise confirm the lights' identity. The court believed that he may have been misled but the negligence of the harbour authority did not exonerate his failure to check his vessel's position by every means at his disposal. The court felt that in the circumstances he should have laid off until morning.

They apportioned one-third of the blame to the Harbour Authority, and two-thirds to the barge's skipper.

IDENTIFY A DINGHY (1)

a Albacore
b Heron
c GP 14
d Kestrel
e Finn
f Fireball
g Bosun
h Cherub
i Contender
j Flying Fifteen
k Laser
l Graduate
m Javelin
n International Moth
o Merlin Rocket
p Osprey
q Marlin
r Mirror
s Sailfish
t Topper

ODD MAN OUT

1. The New England dory – all the rest are British Isles fishing craft
2. The South American pampero – the others are Mediterranean winds
3. The timber hitch – the rest are knots
4. Ghosting – the only one which describes moving a vessel under sail
5. Bradford – the remainder are RNLI lifeboat designs
6. Blooper or cruising chute – the only yacht sail, the rest are sails from square-rig ships
7. Sentinel – the name given to the weight put on an anchor cable to increase catenary

8 Forrestal – all the others are admirals who have had capital ships named after them. Forrestal was US Navy Secretary
9 Humphrey Barton – the rest are designers
10 Clinker – all the others have smooth, unribbed surfaces
11 *Club Mediterranée* – she came in second, the remainder were first home in OSTAR
12 Scuppers – the remainder are below the waterline plumbing

WE'VE GOT PROBLEMS (6)

The only possibility of reaching the man in the dinghy would be to buoy a line with fenders, or better still lightweight plastic cannisters, and let it float down with the wind. Use something the man can easily grab on the end.

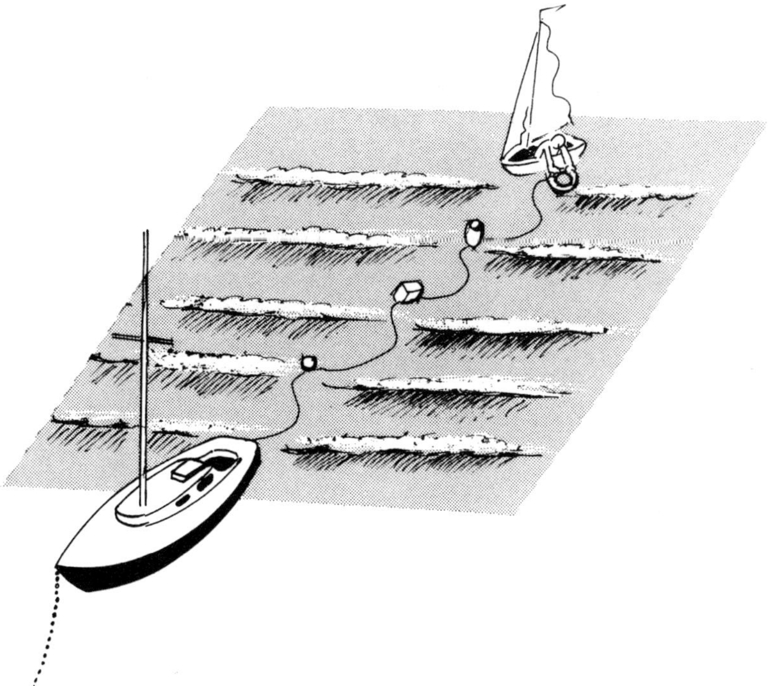

CROSSWORD (2)

1 J	2 E	S	3 T	E	4 R		5 B	Y	N	6 G
	D		R		H					I
	7 D	R	O	G	U	E				N
	I		T		M			8 S		G
9 M	E	S	S		10 B	11 A	R	Q	U	E
	S			12 J		R		U		R
13 C		14 A	B	E	A	M		A		B
A		B		T		A		L		R
15 R	O	A	D	S		16 D	U	L	S	E
G		C		A		A				A
17 O	A	K	U	M						D

SHIPS OF EXPLORATION AND DISCOVERY

1 *Nina, Pinta, Santa Maria*
2 HMS *Beagle*
3 USS *Nautillus*
4 *Ra*
5 *Resolution* and *Adventure*
6 *Endurance*
7 *Argo*
8 *Calypso*
9 *Brendan*
10 *Gjøa*
11 *Trinidad*
12 HMS *Challenger*
13 *Investigator*
14 *Speedwell*

SOMETHING COCK-EYED SOMEWHERE

1 Eling
2 Hamble River entrance
3 Newtown River
4 Calshot
5 Lymington River
6 Langstone Harbour
7 Keyhaven
8 Cowes
9 Wootton Creek
10 Christchurch

WORKING SAIL FROM WHERE?

1 Chasse Marée – French trawler or mackerel line fisherman
2 Arab dhow
3 (River) Humber keel
4 Baltic ketch
5 Portuguese muletta
6 Norfolk wherry
7 Dutch tjalk
8 Spanish felucca
9 Maltese ferilla
10 Norwegian lifeboat
11 Egyptian dahabiyah
12 Greek caique

CROSSWORD (3)

1 M	E	2 O	N		3 S	T	4 R	O	5 P
A		I			P		O		R
6 R	O	L	L	E	R		W		A
I		S			I		L		M
N		K		7 A	N	S	O	8 N	
E		I			G		C	E	
9 S	10 O	N	11 A	R		12 S	K	E	G
	R					I		D	
13 F	L	A	R	E		14 R	O	L	L
	O					E		E	
	15 P	E	N	N	A	N	T	S	

GUESSTIMATE

1 You won't be going out; the wind speed is between 15 and 20 knots.
2 From the top of the mast you can see approximately twice as far, about 6.3 miles.
3 If the bow wave can be seen then the ferry is on the horizon, not below it; distance about 3 miles. The service speed of these ships is about 20 knots which means they cover a mile in 3 minutes. You have nearly ten minutes to cover yourself.
4 You will need a minimum of six 40-gallon oil drums. The buoyancy of a drum or any closed vessel equals the cubic content in gallons multiplied by ten less the weight of the drums themselves. Six times 40 gallons will give 2,400lbs of positive buoyancy.

5 Your rope is quite sufficiently strong. A 10mm nylon rope can hold 4,590lbs.
6 All knots weaken rope but none so severely as an overhand knot which reduces the rope's strength by 40 per cent.
7 You are well clear of the rock. Facial features, eyebrow line and mouth do not become visible until about 100 metres away.
8 You should turn the boat around on a reciprocal course, you have overshot the buoy by 3 minutes or 2 cables.
9 A man is reckoned to be able to pull about 120lbs. Two men therefore can lift 240lbs. Multiply this by the number of parts of rope (4) and it gives a lifting capacity of 960lbs. With friction loss taken into account you will not have sufficient power. You will need either a six-part tackle, or more friends.
10 The recommended CQR anchor weight for a boat of this size is 35lbs. Rope manufacturer's tables suggest 16mm nylon rope.

WE'VE GOT PROBLEMS (7)

1 Grapple for the crab line and bring a bight aboard
2 Take the bight forward and anchor the boat with this. She will now turn into the wind and tide
3 Providing sufficient slack has been left the weight will now be off the propeller and an attempt can be made to clear it
4 A first method to try is using the dinghy to achieve a direct pull while the propeller is reversed manually. The weight of wind and tide on the dinghy should pull the turns off

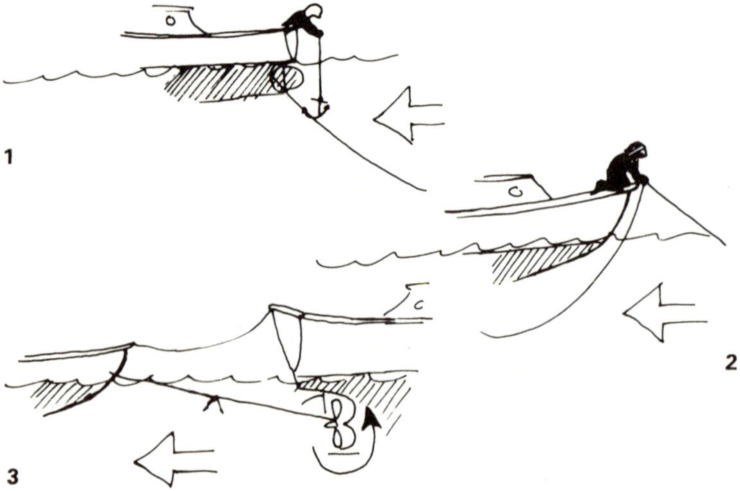

SPOT THE LIGHTHOUSE

1 Fastnet
2 Needles
3 Beachy Head
4 Old Head of Kinsale
5 Dungeness
6 Eddystone Rocks
7 Royal Sovereign
8 Casquets
9 Portland Bill
10 Wolf Rock

WATER WISDOM

1 53 feet
2 It would supply the world's electricity needs for 5 years
3 To latitude 31°N, or just south of Bermuda
4 80 per cent
5 Surtsey
6 Yes, on account of its higher salt content (3.8 per cent compared with 3.6 per cent in the Atlantic and Caribbean)
7 The worst tsunami recorded reached speeds of 490 mph
8 7 miles (the Challenger Trench off Guam)
9 112 feet
10 Between 2,100 and 2,300
11 Soluble salts which over the years have leached out from the land
12 An estimated 60,000 years
13 60 feet
14 The Caspian Sea
15 25 feet
16 True; the collision of subterranean belts of warm and cold water meeting over peaks create monumental disturbances many times more ferocious than wind driven storms
17 Ten years

IN YOUR JUDGEMENT (7)

After some deliberation the court decided that an anchored boat was considered moored within the terms of law. Furthermore, that while certainly there *is* public right of way in tidal waters the situation is analagous to the public right of way on a highway and is not without its limitation. For example, it was perfectly in order to walk down the highway but that did not mean one could lie down and sleep. It was permissible to stop and unload a van but it was not permitted to sell items from the van. In other words a right of way was literally what it said, a passage not permanent occupation. The man lost his appeal.

IN YOUR JUDGEMENT (8)

The judge told the jury that the true commercial value on the market must have a certain elasticity but for the yacht to increase its value by this amount did seem to be stretching credulity to the breaking point. The jury held that there was a case of overvaluation which although not fraudulent did nullify the insurance within the policy terms. The insurance company did not have to pay.

DEAR MUM, IT'S A . . . !

1 Sagged
2 Tender
3 Yawed
4 Cavitated
5 Griped
6 Reefed
7 Weather helm
8 In stays, in irons
9 Pay off
10 Pounding
11 Panting
12 Heave-to
13 Leeway
14 Fore-reaching
15 Windage
16 Broached
17 Distressed British Seaman

YACHTS & YACHTSMEN

1 Chay Blyth
2 Sir Francis Chichester
3 Eric Tabarly
4 H. W. Tilman
5 Joshua Slocum
6 Vito Dumas
7 Sir Thomas Lipton
8 Alain Gerbault
9 H. G. Hasler
10 Dr Peter Pye
11 Susan & Eric Hiscock
12 Dame Naomi James
13 Beryl & Miles Smeeton
14 Sir Alec Rose
15 John H. Illingworth
16 R. T. McMullen
17 Bernard Moitessier
18 Harry Pidgeon
19 John Guzzwell
20 Nick Keig
21 Phil Weld
22 David Lewis
23 Sir Tommy Sopwith
24 Sir Henry Seagrave
25 Humphrey Barton

CHOICE OF CUT

He wants sail numbers **2**, **4** and **7**

IN YOUR JUDGEMENT (9)

They were correct. An appeal court decided that the craft was not covered as the Channel Islands were not a part of the United Kingdom.

IDENTIFY A DINGHY (2)

a Tornado
b Optimist
c Mermaid
d Swift
e Wayfarer
f Skipper
g Solo
h Scorpion
i OK
j Snipe
k Tempest
l Bonito
m Hornet
n Firefly
o Condor
p Vagabond
q Cadet
r Seafly
s Unicorn
t Enterprise

WHAT'S WRONG HERE?

1 Jib not hoisted fully; it has a baggy luff
2 Jib sheet led too far aft causing sail to be stretched on the foot and distorted in the leech
3 Boat has not been checked and made ready for sea; the forehatch cover has been left off which could lead to flooding; a fender has been left hanging and a warp trails over the side where it could snarl the propeller
4 The radar reflector is hoisted incorrectly
5 A halyard is free
6 She exhibits no ensign, as she is required to do by law
7 She is under engine and should therefore show a black cone, another legal requirement
8 The mainsail foot has been stretched too far aft and the leech is distorted
9 A crew member is sitting on the rail – something which only fools and first trippers do
10 She appears to have no lifebuoy
11 No sail number or large name on her side which HM Coastguard recommend for clear identification
12 No sign of an anchor ready to let go in emergency
13 No lifejackets worn by the crew

FLAG ETIQUETTE

1 *Incorrect;* the ensign is hoisted at 8am local time, and ensigns are not flown but worn
2 *Incorrect;* when racing a vessel must hoist her racing flag in place of her burgee and ensign. If she retires the ensign and burgee are worn
3 *Incorrect;* only British subjects may wear the red ensign afloat
4 *Correct*
5 *Incorrect;* the blue ensign can only be worn when the owner of the warrant is aboard
6 *Correct;* naval ships in action wear several ensigns. Ships leaving harbour may briefly exhibit two ensigns as they lower one at the ensign staff and hoist one at the gaff which is where the ensign is worn at sea. Yachts showing courtesy ensigns also have two ensigns, and so may vessels dressed overall
7 *Incorrect;* the saluted vessel must hoist her flag before you
8 *Correct*
9 *Incorrect;* you do not salute the Trinity House yacht with her defaced white ensign, nor yachts of the Royal Yacht Squadron even though they wear the white ensign
10 *Correct*
11 *Incorrect;* the maritime flag should be shown
12 *Correct*
13 *Incorrect;* if an owner belongs to more than one club and wishes to wear a hoist of burgees then the senior (or 'Royal') club burgee must be worn at the top
14 *Correct*
15 *Incorrect*
16 *Correct*
17 *Incorrect;* only the ensign is half-masted
18 *Correct*
19 *Correct;* fishing boats have a registered number exhibited and need not comply with the laws concerning the wearing of ensigns
20 *Correct*

WHO ARE THEY?

1 Juan Sebastian Del Cano
2 Uffa Fox
3 Popeye the Sailor
4 Norman Wilkinson
5 Alan Villiers
6 Olin Stephens
7 Sir Cloudesley Shovell
8 Admiral Togo
9 Alain Bombard
10 Arthur Ransome
11 Paul Jones
12 Alain Gerbault
13 Captain Vanderdecken (The Flying Dutchman)
14 Robert Fitzroy
15 Grace Darling

WE'VE GOT PROBLEMS (8)

Start the engine and motor ahead. The breast lines will then act as springs and pull the boat alongside.

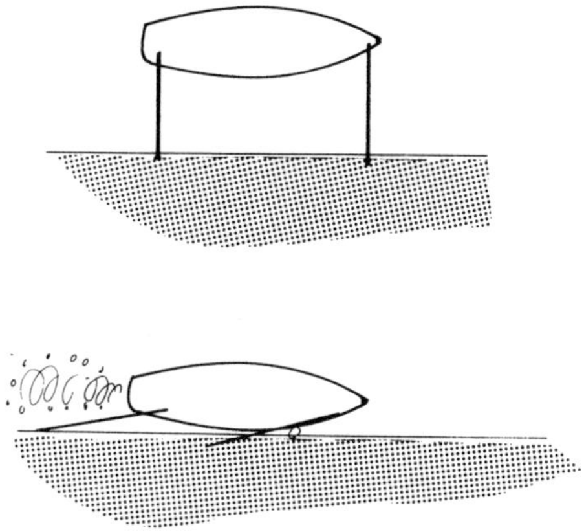

CROSSWORD (4)

		1 M			2 E		3 B	U	N	4 T
5 P	R	A	T	I	Q	U	E			H
R		S			U		6 R	I	G	A
7 O	P	T	I	M	I	S	T			M
T		E			N		H			E
E		R		8 C	O	L	O	U	9 R	S
S			10 C		C		N		O	
11 T	12 H	W	A	R	T				Y	
	I		B		13 I	S	O	B	A	R
	G		I		A				L	
14 C	H	A	N	D	L	E	R		S	

ANIMAL CONNECTIONS

Bass rope (*made from coconut fibre*)
Bee block (*for reefing*)
Beetle (*rigging tool*)
Bulldog grip
Bull rope
Bull's eye

Camel (*kind of wooden fender*)
Cat boat
Cat davit
Catspaw
Cat walk
Cockbill
Cockpit
Cod end (*of a trawl*)
Cod headed (*bluff bowed*)
Cod line
Crab (*catch a crab, rowing*)
Crow foot
Crow jack
Crow's nest

Dog (*pawl*)
Doghouse
Dog watch
Dolphin striker (*on bowsprit*)
Donkey engine
Donkey greaser
Donkey's breakfast

Elephant's trunk (*chain bow fender*)

Fish (*join broken spars together*)
Fish plate

Goose-neck
Goose-wing

Hog (*hull curvature*)
Hogshead
Horse latitudes
Horse (*sheet horse*)
Hounds
Houndsband

Jackass barque

Leg o' mutton (*slang for Bermudian sail*)
Lizard (*short length of rope*)

Mackerel-tailed (*with fine run aft*)
Mole (*harbour protection*)
Monkey block
Monkey island
Monkey jacket
Powder monkey
Monkey's fist
'Monkey' was used by sailors to denote anything small
Mouse (*to secure a block or hook*)
Mosquito boats (*generic term for small, fast craft*)
Mule (*type of fishing boat: large, sharp-sterned coble*)

Otter board (*for trawling*)

Pelican hook
Pigs (*ballast*)

Ram (*bow*)
Ramshorn (*hook*)
Ratline
Rat's tail (*pointing a rope*)
Roach
Round robin

Skylark
Sole (*cabin floor, or small boat*)
Spider
Spider bend

Turtle bag
Turtle deck

Whaler (*whale boat*)
Worm (*worm, parcel and serve*)